INSTITUTES OF THE BEVOLLMAECHTIGTER FUER HOCHFREQUENZ-FORSCHUNG

(PLENIPOTENTIARY FOR HIGH FREQUENCY RESEARCH)

Reported by

W/Cdr. C.P. EDWARDS	M.A.P.
S/Ldr. W.E.J. FARVIS	M.A.P.
Capt. SNOWDEN	M. of S.
Capt. CAPLIN	M. of S.
Lt. REDGEMENT	A.S.E.
Mr HANSEL	T.I.I.C.
Capt. EMPLIN	Br. Army
Mr OMBERG	U.S. Sig. Corps
Mr SODERMAN	O.S.R.D.
Capt. F. BORTHWICK	M. of S.
Mr S.E. TOULMIN	M.A.P.
Lt.Col. R.G. FRIEND	M. of S.
Major W.H. MADDISON	M. of S.
S/Ldr. S. DEVONS	M.A.P.
Mr M.B. GOTTLIEB	O.S.R.D.
S/Ldr. G.C. BARKER	M.A.P.

CIOS Items 1 and 7
Radar and Signals Communications

COMBINED INTELLIGENCE OBJECTIVES SUB-COMMITTEE
G-2 Division, SHAEF (Rear), APO 413

The Naval & Military Press Ltd

Published by

The Naval & Military Press Ltd
Unit 5 Riverside, Brambleside
Bellbrook Industrial Estate
Uckfield, East Sussex
TN22 1QQ England

Tel: +44 (0)1825 749494

www.naval-military-press.com
www.nmarchive.com

*In reprinting in facsimile from the original, any imperfections are inevitably reproduced
and the quality may fall short of modern type and cartographic standards.*

TABLE OF CONTENTS.

Subject. **Page No.**

A. **FERDINAND BRAUN INSTITUTE.**

   REPORT I - Summary of reports on the FBI

      Distribution of sections.   8
      Hotel Post, Brannenburg.   "
      Schloss Pullach.   9
      Irschenberg   "
      Gaisberg   10
      Ismaning   "
      Swifting   "
      Herzogstand.   11

   REPORT II - Survey of German Navigational Aid Systems.

      Before the War   12
      During the War   14
      Developments due to Prof. von Handel's institute.   "
      Work of Dr Plendl's institute.   16
      Reports of German Navigational Aids.   17

   REPORT III - Interrogation of Drs Handel, Kovats and Knoll.

      Interview with Drs Handel and Kovats   18
      Interview with Dr Knoll   "
      Control of Spot size in cathode-ray tubes   19
      Electrically conducting screens for cathode-ray tubes.   20
      Combined Fast and Slow screens.   "
      Measurement of secondary emission from c.r.t. screens.   "
      Image retaining screens   21
      Projection type cathode-ray tubes   "
      Iconoscope Development   22
      Military television systems   "
      Sources of caesium activating material   23
      Getter materials   "
      Glass-metal seals   "
      Time division multiples   "
      Glow-lamp modulators   "
      Light-reflection-reducing films   24
      Coating of searchlight mirrors   "
      Information of interest   25
      Reports from Telefunken, Bad Liebenstein.   26

REPORT IV - Schloss Pullach, Bad Aibling

    Interrogation of Handel, Pfister, Grassmann and Neun
    Interrogation of Labus and Kluge
    Gas Discharge at Centimetre Wavelengths.
    Spark Characteristics in gas-filled 3-electrode tubes
    The Bildwandler as a light amplifier
    Glow-cathode heated by burning
    Heat retaining cathode construction
    On Contact-lighting of Carborundum Crystals.

REPORT V - Outstation at Gaisberg

    Propagation measurements
    Detection of shell-bursts
    Communications
    Jamming of H2S
    Future work
    Laboratories
    Documents

REPORT VI - Outstation at Irschenberg

    Erika installation
    Documents
    Recommendations
    Report on propagation by Dr Lehfeldt
    Report on Erika by Gassmann and Neun

REPORT VII - Komet experimental site at Ismaning

    General description
    Errors due to angle of elevation
    Measuring the time-intervals
    Recorder mechanism
    Performance
    Documents
    Sequence

REPORT VIII - Swifting

    Dispersal Stores
    Personnel
    Documents
    Activities
    Equipment
    Target information
    Requests by staff

REPORT IX - Ionospheric recording station at Herzogstand

    Personnel Interrogated   61
    Equipment   62
    Results   63
    Publications   "
    Recommendations   64

B. ERNST ORLICH INSTITUTE.

REPORT I - Projects of the Ernst Orlich Institute.

1.	Mechanical vibrators as filters for harmonics.	65
2.	Extirpation of hum by Mechanical Resonant Filters.	67
3.	Mechanical Resonant Filters, as anti-jamming for Radar.	69
4.	Pulse modulating as a means of removing Radar disturbance due to Window.	70
5.	Guiding beam system at 600/ mc/s for remote controlled Rockets.	72
6.	Measuring in the 500 to 5000 mc/s band.	74
7.	Electric and Magnetic properties measurements up to very high frequencies.	76
8.	Causes of Atmospherics; How to quench them.	77
9.	Additional information on atmospheric electricity.	79
10.	How to use atmospherics for weather forecasts.	80
11.	Dry Textile discharger for planes.	81
12.	Can atmospheric electricity upset the control of projectiles telecontrolled by wires?	82
13.	Limitations of German proximity fuses due to Atmospheric Electricity.	83
14.	Contributions to the knowledge of so called Precipitation Statics.	84
15.	Fundamental Investigations on Magnetically Homing Torpedoes.	85
16.	Magnet proximity release for tank-destroying Rockets fired by planes.	86

17.	Fundamental considerations on magnetic anti-aircraft proximity fuses.	87
18.	Magnetically actuated alarm system for areas to be protected.	88
19.	Magnetic shielding in the low Frequency Range.	89
20.	Stray fields of Transformers and Iron cored coils.	90
21.	Modulation of C.W. Short Wave Transmission in the Propagation Way.	91
22.	C.W. Short Wave Radar.	92
23.	Short Wave proximity fuse.	93
24.	Remote controlled Short Wave Proximity Fuse.	94
25.	Improved Short Wave proximity Fuse.	95
26.	Measuring current and tension distribution in Oscillating bodies.	96
27.	Fundamental wave-lengths of Planes and their quality.	97
28.	Atmospheric radiation as a source of trouble for Long Wave Infra Red.	98
29.	Highly sensitive Thermo elements for Radiation metering with short time lags.	100
30.	Infra Red Mapping equipment.	102
31.	Infra Red Aiming equipment.	104
32.	Thermo-electric Detector as a standard for very high frequencies.	105
33.	Characteristics of Detectors for very high frequencies.	106

34.	Contact potential.	107
35.	Generating Voltmeters.	108
36.	Pulse Transformers.	110
37.	Charging line, Pulse Transformer and Valve load.	111
38.	Pulse Analyser.	112
39.	Highly sensitive D.C. controlling device.	113
40.	Highly sensitive D.C. Measuring Converter.	115
41.	Self balanced Hisentroll as linear D.C. Amplifier.	117
42.	Limitations of the Hisentroll.	118
43.	Vibration proof Hisentroll and Hisenvert.	120
44.	Highly sensitive simple Zero Indicating Device for High Resistance d.c. Measurements.	121
45.	Counter-measures against Homing or Remote Controlled Torpedoes.	123
46.	Excitation of circular cavity Resonators by means of Density modulated beams of slow electrons.	124

REPORT II. - Reports available at C.R.B.   125

C. ERNST LECHER INSTITUTE.

Report I - Technical Report.   162

    Report on preliminary discussion with Dr Plendl   "
    and Dr Häter.
    Report on technical work in progress and completed.   168
    List of personnel.   178
    List of reports prepared by the Institute.   181
    List of reports removed.   183
    List of reports held by Dr Plendl.   187
    List of such reports removed.   189
    Financial position of the Institute.   191

Report II - Interrogation of Dr Plendl on RCM   192

D. ZENTRALVERSUCHSTELLE FÜR H F FORSCHUNG.

    Discussion with Dr Breuning and General Appreciation.   197
    Report on technical work in progress and completed.   200
    List of personnel.
    List of reports issued and there being forwarded
    to CIOS.   207
    List of scientific personnel in the Bad Aibling area.   209
    Action taken.   210

E. GEORG SIMON INSTITUTE.   211

F. REICHSTELLE FÜR H F FORSCHUNG HAMBURG.   213

G. REICHSTELLE FÜR H F FORSCHUNG SCHLESWIG.   214

A. **FERDINAND BRAUN INSTITUTE.**

REPORT I.

Summary of Reports on the

FERDINAND-BRAUN INSTITUTE

Reichstelle für Hochfrequenz Forschung E.V.

Distribution of Institutes:

Head Office: Hotel Post. Brannenburg am Inn.

Director: Prof. Dr. Ing. Freih. von Handel.

Ground-wave Division.

Schloss Pullach, Nr. Bad Aibling.	Div. Leader Dr. Pfister.
Gaisberg, Nr Salzburg.	Group Leader. Dr. Hähnel.
Irschenberg, Nr. Bad Aibling.	Group Leader. Dr Gassmann.

Skywave Division.

Schwifting, Nr Landsberg/Lech.	Div. Leader, Dr Crone.
Herzogstand, Nr Kochel.	Group Leader. Dipl. Phys. Petersen.
Ismaning, Nr Erding.	Group Leader. Dr Friedl.

These Institutes have most of their Staff and Equipment intact. The activities of resident "Visitors" from other Establishments are mentioned in this summary and in the detailed reports.

(1) **HOTEL POST. BRANNENBURG.**

Prof. v. Handel arranged full cooperation and supplied copies of all the reports of the F-B Institutes. He also accompanied the investigators to three of the stations.

Handel gave a brief history of all the navigational systems, which has been supplemented and reported by

S/L Farvis. Graf Soden v. Fraunhofen was absent during the visit. He is a mathematician, and right-hand man to Handel in forecasting the probable results of experimental projects.

Dr Kovats is a competent man, but is doing technical administration and organisation only.

Dr Aesendorf and Dr Mann also do stores purchasing and detail administration.

No experimental work is done here, and there is no equipment.

An important guest, Prof. Knoll, formerly in charge of Telefunken Television labs., and with a wide knowledge of vacuum-tube science was interviewed and later taken to Bad Liebenstein. The report is by Hansell and Snowden.

(2) SCHLOSS PULLACH.

Direct-ray or ground-wave navigation systems development including long-period performance tests formed the main work of this station. More recent work has been a study of the limits of accuracy of radar range measurement using transmitter responder equipment. The work is incomplete. Work on the jamming of "ground-seeing" equipment had commenced but was in an elementary stage. An investigation had been carried out on the performance and jammability of the Bernhard-Bernhardine azimuth beacon system developed by Lorenz.

The chief personnel are Dr Pfister, Dr Breuninger and Dr Wegmann.

Personnel not belonging to the station were Dr Labus, a Klystron and wave-guide expert ex-Telefunken, and Prof. Werner Kluger. They were interviewed by Hansell and Snowden who have reported. The report on Schloss Pullach is by Lt. Redgment.

(3) IRSCHENBERG.

This is the site of a complete "Erica" installation giving coverage of the greater part of Germany in conjunction with a second station near Vienna. The station uses six aerial systems, each fed by a 5 kw transmitter, and is highly accurate "Superortung". A coarse pattern is given by two aerials spaced 2 λ and a fine pattern by aerials spaced 27 λ The complete aircraft installation for position finding uses four receivers type E.Bl.3h (30 - 33.3 Mc/s) and two indicators. Later development on Erica for installation in France and Denmark was done by Dr Goldman of Lorenz, who has been interviewed at Landshut. These stations were not put into use due to ease of jamming.

The personnel at Irschenberg are <u>Dr Gassmann</u> and <u>Dipl. Ing. Neun</u> with some five assistants.

The laboratories contained test equipment of good quality in a wide range.

The station also housed <u>Dr Lehfeld</u> of Siemens, who had a laboratory and ample equipment. He was working on the conversion of a Feuermolch jammer, using the L.D.9 ceramic triode for use in propagation research. The report is by S/L Farvis.

(4) <u>GAISBERG</u>.

This station on the peak of the Gaisberg is devoted to radar propagation measurements, reflection coefficient measurements and H2S jamming. Work is continuing on reflection from the blast wave from bombs and shells.

The station has Wurzburg and Freya equipment and is incidentally an important junction point on the military 50 cm radio teleprinter network.

Of a total staff of 15, (formerly 21), the important men are <u>Dr Hähnel</u>, <u>Dr Jacob</u> and <u>Dipl. Ing. Englebrecht</u>. The report is by S/L Farvis.

(5) <u>ISMANING</u>

Komet experimental site. Accuracy experiments by Dr Pirkheim under direction of Dr Pfister.

(6) <u>SWIFTING</u>.

The principal work of this station was the analysis of "Komet" long range navigation system performance over a long period. Other work has included research on anti-interference radar, synchronisation schemes for Loran, D/F on kilometer waves, the discharge of aircraft static charges by addition of suitable compounds to the fuel, and the amplitude modulation of cm pulses by gas tubes. Reports received cover practically all this work.

The labs. are well equipped, and a dispersal of good quality H.F. and V.H.F. Lab. equipment exists at Schonberg on the Ammer See.

Of a total staff of some 40 persons, the principal names are Dr Crone, Dr Martin, Dr Mitzaika, Dipl. Phys. Dessauer, Dr Friedl, Dipl. Ing Hummrick and Dipl. Ing. Landstorfer.

The report is by W/C C.P. Edwards.

(7) HERZOGSTAND.

This station carries out routine ionospheric soundings for use in forecasting operational frequencies for Service use. The results, along with those of 14 other stations were reported to a central agency. Before the war the station was operated by Prof. Zenneck of the T.H. Munich, with Dr Gubau, now at Jena.

The equipment used since 1937 is entirely automatic covering 1 - 10 Mc/s with two horizontal dipoles. The p.r.f. is 50 c/s and duration some 100 μ-sec. Film records exist covering the last 14 years, and there is little doubt that this station should be kept in operation.

All documents other than the films have been taken to Great Baddow, England, by Maj. Kojan of the U.S. Signal Corps.

The station is now in charge of Dipl. Phys. Petersen with Dr Eyfrig and some 5 other persons in all.

The detailed report is by Farvis and Regment.

C.P. EDWARDS.
31 May, 1945
at Munich.

REPORT II.

FERDINAND-BRAUN INSTITUTE.
(REICHSTELLE FÜR HOCHFREQUENZTECHNIK).

Date: May 25th 1945.

Investigators:

W/C. Edwards.	R.A.E.
S/Ldr. Parvis.	T.R.E.
Capt. Snowden	R.R.D.E.
Capt. Caplin	S.R.D.E.
Lt. Redgment	A.S.E.
Mr Hansel	R.C.A.

Personnel Interrogated –

Prof. Dr. Ing. Freiherr Paul von Handel,
Dr Kovats.
Prof. Knoll (Telefunkenguest)

Address: The H.Q. of this institute, which has a number of outstations, is at Gasthof Post Hotel, Brannenburg/Inn.

The interrogations at Gasthof Post were done in two parts; Capt. Snowden and Mr Hansel interviewed Prof. Knoll while the rest of the party interviewed Prof. v. Handel and Dr Kovats. This report deals only with the latter part in which Prof. v. Handel was asked to give a survey of the German navigational aid systems: the first part is reported separately.

1. Survey of German Navigational Aid Systems.

Before the War. As far back as 1934 Prof. v. Handel claims to have proposed the Erika C.W. Hyperbola system on 40 Mc/s, and started to build it at an airfield in Berlin. Because of the magnitude of the undertaking, the small staff, the limited funds and few aircraft, it had to be dropped.

Then there was a phase of rotating beacons between 1937 and 1939. Prof. v. Handel's team worked on the development of <u>Dora.</u> This was a simple rotating beacom with a <u>simple</u> polar diagram. It consisted of a transmitting 4-aerial buried U Adcock with quarter wavelength spacing and rotation by means of a goniometer. The system was for 6 Mc/s and was erected at Ismaning, N.E. of Munich. It was subject to the same errors as a receiving Adcock of the same type and was therefore not an accurate system.

In parallel with this von Handel development, Dr Plendl, at Rechlin, was working on a rotating beacon where the direction of the aerials was indicated by the frequency of a tone whose frequency was varied continuously throughout the cycle of rotation. It called for a very precise frequency bridge apparatus in the aircraft and largely on these grounds was dropped in 1939.

In order to overcome the errors in the Dora system due primarily to the mixed returns from the ionosphere, Prof. v. Handel, in conjunction with Dr. Runge of Telefunken worked on the first pulse navigational system called <u>Ingolstadt.</u> Handel claimed that this was similar to Loran, but this is not strictly true. Comparison between "left" and "right" of the equisignal path from a "split" polar diagram was obtained by observation of the amplitude of the two sets of pulses, rather than path difference. Observations on the accuracy of the system were made at long range around the "equisignal" path. It was found there was no such clearly defined path. The important observation was made, however, that by counting over long periods at the various points across the equizone then the positions Left, Right and Centre, could be found with very good accuracy and consistently, by taking the average of a number of observations at each point. Having discovered this fact they were led back to C.W. systems due to the simplicity of equipment in the aircraft, with the firm conviction that ionospheric fluctuations were not deleterious to sky wave systems, providing integration over a period was done. All the later sky wave systems from this Institute therefore incorporated

recording type indicating systems rather than
C.R.T's. Ingolstadt was abandoned.

The firm of Lorenz had for several years before the
war been developing E-T Blind Approach beam systems.

2. <u>During the War</u>. When the war started there were two
apparently conflicting navigational aid requirements
put to the scientists by General Martini.
The Luftwaffe wanted an accurate long range navigational
system which was available to all aircraft simultaneously;
at the same time they required a super-accurate
bombing aid system which could select individual
targets. (Goering did not want "boxes" at all).
Work on these different methods was proceeding in
parallel at the two principal navigational-aid
establishments; viz. under Prof. von Handel at
D.V.L. and under Dr Plendl at Rechlin. Lorenz or
Telefunken were called on in both cases to build the
final equipment and these firms often added ideas
of their own before the schemes were finished.
These parallel developments in the first three
years of the war can most conveniently be treated
under two headings, viz. those by Prof. von Handel
and those by Dr Plendl.

<u>Developments due to Prof. von Handel's Institute.</u>

About 1940 the first <u>Komet</u> system was developed by
Dr Pfister. It was really an improvement of Dora,
to include a recording type of display as indicated
from Ingolstadt, together with a large aerial
separation (10λ) which earlier work had indicated led
to greater accuracy. The new system was likely to be
a long time under development because there were
likely to be many unknown and fundamental new factors
involved. So, to satisfy the urgent Luftwaffe
requirements <u>Electra</u> was built by Lorenz. It embodied
those principles of Komet which were certain and
was given a frequency where it was reasonably certain
that there would be no propagational errors. It was
built for a wavelength of 1000 metres, using a three
aerial system of 6λ aperture. It was intended only
as a ground-wave day system, and provided a series

of "laid" beams along which aircraft could fly over England. Being covered by Elektra, Komet was able to go ahead as a long term research item to discover ultimate accuracies of long range sky wave C.W. systems. A permanent long base line from Berlin to Italy and Sicily was set up for experimental propagation experiments, while other developments on practical systems were proceeding, incorporating the results obtained.

One of the principal errors appreciated at an early date was that owing to the angle of elevation of the sky wave the equisignal surface at azimuths away from the normal to the array was a hyperboloid. To avoid this, the first practical Komet scanned only a very small arc ($\pm 1.1/2$ degs) at a time and had several sets of aerials in order to cover a useful geographical sector. Such a multi-aerial Komet, with 4λ spacing was installed at Bordeaux, though it was never used operationally because of the troubles in feeding the complicated aerial system.

In the meantime Elektra, a fixed beam system, had been extended by Lorenz along the Komet lines, into a long wave navigational system of the rotating beacon type - Sonne. Sonne was limited in its swing to about 60 degs, and was also only suitable for day use with any degree of accuracy. A chain of Sonne stations was built. The V.H.F. night equivalent of Sonne called Mond was proposed by Lorenz but was never built. Later came Goldsonne (proposed by Dr Goldmann of Lorenz) which was a multi-aerial system (not so complicated as Komet) to cover a much larger angle.

There was another line of development which can also be traced back to Komet. The Navy (NVK, Dr Bachem) and Telefunken produced a rotating beam system called Wullenwever, which was started as a sort of M.U.S.A. beamed receiving system able to be swung over 360 degs, and consisted of a full circle of closely spaced aerials. Prof. von Handel saw the possibilities of such a system as an improvement of Komet, and suggested it should be modified to give a "split" pattern and used as a transmitting beacon to give 360 degs. coverage. Dr Goldmann of Lorenz added other details and at a conference held in July 1944 it was decided to build a new system Goldwever. It has not been produced yet.

The present Komet allows quite large swings, the errors due to obliquity being allowed for by there being two "base lines" inclined at an angle of, say, 30 degs. Observations are made (by a recorder) on both systems for alternate minute intervals, and the correct azimuth is given from a chart which gives the projection on the ground of the point of intersection of the two equisignal hyperboloids.

Full reports of the Komet and other systems are given in a BHF document.

Work of Dr Plendl's Institute.

Immediately after Dunkirk, June 1940, Dr Plendl was called on, at Rechlin, to produce within three months an accurate bombing aid for bombers to use in the winter 1940/41 over England. Within three months Dr Plendl's group had an X-gerät equipment made in the laboratory and being flown experimentally (he has described how it needed careful nursing), and by November 3 or 4 sets were flying over England, with the scientists waiting at the aerodromes to keep the sets serviceable.

Within a month or two (i.e. still 1940) the first Y Gerät (beam and ranging) was tried out and experimental flights continued until February, when KG26 took over. Unfortunately on their first regular operation the British jammed their equipment and Y had a very bad start, from which the bombers never really recovered.

Lorenz had been before the war developing E-T system such as now used by the Germans and ourselves for Blind Approach, and by 1940 had a number of Knickebein fixed beam stations providing beam approach for bombers to Britain.

Early in 1943 the AM decided that CW navigational aids were no use for war as they were so easily jammed. As a result of this the Erika stations in France were never switched on, though Erika 3 and 4 at Irschenberg and Tulln were allowed to go ahead for experimental and training purposes.

Effort was then directed to development of pulse systems which were Trüke (use of our Gee) Egon and Baldur (Egon in reverse, using SN2).

Until these systems were ready, the Lorenz talking beacon Hermine, and the Telefunken equipment Bernhard and Bernhardine were used as they might be difficult to jam.

The Allied jamming of the C.W. aids was most successful. The London area, Southampton and Portsmouth were badly jammed. Plymouth was not so serious. The Germans could never understand why we did not jam Sonne; they decided perhaps we were using it ourselves.

The people of the Ferdinand Braun Institute have no doubt in their minds that their best navigational aid and the best system for peace-time work is Erika, giving 0.02 degs. accuracy over 500 Km. Some notes from the Erika station are attached to this report.

Reports on German Navigational Aids.

1. "Goldwever" (Munich CIOS ref. IIIc/3055).

2. "Beschreibung des Erika-Varfahrens" (Superortung)
    Institut für Elektrophysik Adlershof 26.5.1943.
    (Munich CIOS ref. IIIc/3047)

3. Deutsche Luftfahrtforschung
    Untersuchungen u Mitteilen Nr 802/1
    (Munich CIOS Ref. No IIIc/3031).
    Nr 802/2
    (Munich CIOS Ref. No IIIc/3030).

S/Ldr Farvis.

R E P O R T   I I I.

Names of Investigators.

                  Captain M. Snowden   R.R.D.E.
                  Mr C.W. Hansell   T.I.C.

These two accompanied Wing Commander Edwards, Lt. Regment, Capt. Caplin, and S/Ldr Farvis, whose interest was mainly navigational.

Place visited.   Brannenberg headquarters of Ferdinand Braun Institute, an establishment directed by Prof. Dr Baron von Handel, assisted by Dr Kovats.

Persons Interviewed.

            Dr Handel, Dr Kovats and Dr Knoll.

Interview with Drs Handel and Kovats.

Drs Handel and Kovats very briefly described the organisation and the work of the Ferdinand Braun organisation which embraces a number of laboratories, experimental stations working on fundamental physical research, radio propagation and radio navigational aids.

Dr Handel provided a list of reports covering the work of the Institute since its organisation. This list was turned over to group leader Edwards. After a brief discussion the party split up and Dr Knoll was interviewed by Snowden and Hansell.

Interview with Dr Knoll.

Dr Knoll had worked with Telefunken, had been a Professor of physics at Technische Hochschule in Berlin. His line of work had been primarily television tubes and related subjects. He has been visited frequently before the war by Dr V.H. Zworykin of RCA. His laboratories originally were at Berlin but with the advance of the Russians they were evacuated to Bad Liebenstein, near Eisenach.

While away on a trip to Berlin he was cut off by the allied advancing armies and was unable to return to Liebenstein. He then made his way to Brannenberg and attached himself to von Handel. Since that time he has had no information concerning what has happened at Liebenstein.

We obtained from Dr Knoll a list of projects with which he had been concerned and a list of his most prominent collaborators. A copy of his list will be attached.

1. <u>Control of spot size in Cathode Ray Tubes.</u>

In general this type of work was carried on in detail by Dr Gundert of Telefunken and by Dr Hochenberg at Physikalische Institute at Göttingen.

An improved type of screen for reducing spot size was obtained by Dr Hochenberg by burning zinc in a Bunsen flame in air to produce zinc oxide which was allowed to deposit on a glass screen to a thickness just sufficient to absorb nearly all the impinging electrons of the electron beam. Any greater thickness, or a screen in the form of particles would cause a spraying out of primary or secondary electrons in a manner to increase the excited area.

Dr Gundert, we understand, was concerned with attempts to reduce the spot size by study of light phenomena in the fluorescent screens. Apparently the technique of using very thin evaporated screens was the most effective expedient for reducing spreading of light. In other words thin screen reduce light spreading as well as electron spreading.

When questioned Dr Knoll said that he knew of no attempts to reduce spot size by putting light absorbing material in the screens.

2. Electrically conducting screens for Cathode Ray Tubes.

Dr Knoll said that fairly good results had been obtained in reducing unwanted variations in sensitivity and loss of light output caused by unequal and insufficient screen potentials, caused by uneven or insufficient secondary electron emission. This had been done by making the screen conducting without at the same time causing a substantial loss of light due to the presence of the conducting material.

The process consisted of forming the fluorescent screen, according to prior practice, coating with gelatine just sufficient to fill all interstices, evaporating aluminium upon the gelatine treated surface to make a smooth aluminium surface, barely thick enough to result in final adequate conductivity.

During normal baking of the tube to about 400 degs. C the gelatine was automatically removed, leaving the extremely thin aluminium conductor.

3. Combined fast and slow screens.

Dr Gundert was said to have worked on the development of double screen tubes intended to obtain a differential effect between relatively stationary and moving objects. One purpose was to make it easier to distinguish between "window" type radar interference and a rapidly moving aircraft.

4. Measurements of secondary emission from C.R.T. screen.

A project of measuring secondary emission ratio of screens of cathode ray tubes was carried out using extremely thin fluorescent materials, barely thick enough to absorb impinging electrons, which were deposited on a metal surface (Chromium). This expedient provided sufficient conductivity through the screens for making measurements. Secondary emission ratios ranging up to 10 to 1 were measured.

It has been suggested that the combination of very thin fluorescent coatings on metal surfaces might be one good way to make secondary emissive surfaces for electron-current multi-pliers.

5. Image retaining screens.

A promising but unfinished development was that of providing light valve-type image-reproducing screens of potassium chloride, similar in principle to light valves developed by Schophony Ltd. These screens were scanned by a modulated electron beam and were darkened more or less in proportion to charge deposited in the screen at each point. The darkening effect would remain for periods of time ranging up to hours, thus forming a more or less permanent record, which could be established by a single frame or passage of the electron beam over the screen.

The record could be erased by passing a current through a thin transparent tungsten film on which the screen was deposited. The wipe out, we understand, was accomplished primarily due to temperature use of the screen.

Dr Knoll was of the opinion, that this development was not promising for television application but had advantages for some military applications, particularly where continuous transmission would be an aid to the enemy in locating the transmitting equipment.

6. Projection type Cathode Ray Tubes.

An interesting type of Cathode ray tube for projecting images optically on an outside screen was developed in which the screen was formed on a Fernico surface which also was part of the outside envelope of the tube so that it could be adequately cooled. The Fernico was chromium plated and then coated with zinc and cadmium sulphide. The chromium was required to prevent chemical re-action between the Fernico and the screen material.

7. Iconoscope Development.

This development appears to have been carried out in detail by Dr Hass at Schmalkalden near Liebenstein. He has worked iconoscope screens made of semiconducting materials such as copper oxide and lead sulphide and has obtained sensitivities ranging up to 10 times that of the ordinary Iconoscope as known to him. This type of screen gives trouble because the response characteristics do not remain constant, and there is a tendency toward long time delay in response so that it does not seem very promising for television.

The screens of semiconducting material operate on a principle of varying secondary emission ratio in response to impinging light. The images formed by the light tend to be retained for a considerable time but may be erased by exposure to radiations of a somewhat longer wavelength (not infra-red).

Work has been done on supericonoscopes which employ translucent photo cathodes and electron images on a second surface which is scanned by an electron beam, usually using magnetic focussing. Increases in sensitivity up to about 5 to 1 were obtained as compared with the simple iconoscope.

A detail expedient used to improve some iconoscopes was the use of a lens moulded onto the glass envelope. Another was the use of sand-blasting of the iconoscope screen surfaces to improve contrast and definition.

8. Military television systems.

Prof. Dr Fritz Schröter of Telefunken has been in charge of development of at least some of the complete television systems for military applications. He is now at Liebenstein, Near Eisenach, although most Telefunken people are in Blankenberg near Rudolstadt or in Berlin. Dr Knoll understood that television equipment on a flying bomb had been successful in sinking an allied ship at Salerno. The bomb transmitted vision from itself back to a control station from which the flight of the bomb was radio controlled.

9. Sources of caesium activitating material.

Dr Thiele, now at Liebenstein, is familiar with methods of releasing caesium in tubes. Usually Caesium chloride and aluminium powder are mixed and heated to reduce the chloride. Some special mechanical tricks for handling the process apparently have been worked out but were not described.

10. Getter materials.

This type of work has been handled by Dr Statz of Telefunken, in Berlin; Dr Knoll was not familiar with it.

11. Glass-metal seals.

Developments of the technique of sealing glass to metal has been carried out by Dr Espe for Siemens at Rochlitz on Yser, near Karlsbad. For production purposes use has been made of lead-in wires of Krupp V_2A steel.

12. Time-division multiples.

Dr Knoll and his associates had developed cathode ray tubes with multiple anodes for time-division multiples. Dr Roosenstein, last known to be at Nauen, Near Berlin, (Berge) has worked out complete time division multiple systems.

13. Glow-lamp modulators.

Glow-lamp modulators have been developed which provide 70% to 80% audio modulation of 6 cm wave length radiation, 10 milli-watts carrier power with 0.1 as much modulating power as the controlled power. These modulators comprised a d.c. glow-discharge lamp so operated that

that electrode area covered by the glow was less
than 100%. The area covered by glow was then
modulated by modulating the d.c. current.
Only the negative electrode glow was used for
modulating purposes. The lamps were filled with
neon or argon at about 10 millimetres pressure.
1 milliampere of control current would control
10 milliwatts of radio frequency power.

The glow lamps were inserted inside wave-guides
conveying the r.f. power to be radiated and varied
the loss by absorption (and perhaps reflection).
It was stated that maximum modulation frequencies
up to 100,000 cycles were possible.

Complete communications systems using this type
of modulator have been developed. One very
interesting type employs a central transmitting
and receiving station associated a number of
slave stations. The slave stations have no sources
of radio frequency energy of their own but
retransmit power which is modulated by glow tube
modulators before retransmission. Thereby a
form of modulated reflection back to the central
station is provided. This is said to result in
an economy of equipment and power requirements
for some applications.

14. Light reflection reducing films.

Dr Hass has done research and development in
the field of evaporated films for reducing light
reflection from glass. He has had good results
with films of titanium dioxide which when
evaporated at a correct temperature and condensed
at another correct temperature gives films of
substantially correct refractive index.

15. Coating of searchlight mirrors.

An important invention and development by
Dr Hass has been the method of providing searchlight
mirrors in which an evaporated aluminium surface
is covered by a protective evaporated quartz
surface.

In carrying out this process the mirror surface is first made superclean by a glow discharge in low pressure gas, then, while this is maintained at 40 to 50 degs. C. in a high vacuum, aluminium is evaporated from molybdenum boats, heated by 500,000 amperes of low voltage, low frequency current. After aluminium of suitable thickness is obtained quartz is evaporated, to give a layer about 1 micron in thickness, using another set of boats in the same manner. This process has been used on mirrors up to 5 metres diameter, which required quite large vessels and large vacuum pumps. The pumps were supplied by Leybolds-Nachfolger, now in Andreasberg near Göttingen.

It is understood that the mirrors are being produced by Siemens and Hergens-Hannau near Frankfurt.

16. <u>Information of interest.</u>

(a) Dr Heil is probably now at Constance on Bodensee, and has been working on Klystron type tubes. Dr Weisflug is working on similar problems.

(b) Dr Bechmann has been working on quartz crystals at Berlin.

(c) Dr Weiss of the Deutsche Reichspost is near Constance working on secondary emission amplifiers.

(d) Gudden now at Erlangen, formerly at Physical Institute in Prague, has been working on infra-red sensitive cells, using semiconductors.

(e) Schott at Jena has developed a very good type of glass for passing ultraviolet light.

Report written by
Snowden and Hansell.

SOME REPORTS FROM TELEFUNKEN-LABORATORIES F 6 BAD LIEBENSTEIN (Prof. Knoll.)

(Collaborators: Dr Wendl, Dr Theile,
   Dr Gundert, Dr Hachenberg)

1. **Limit of resolving power of cathode ray tubes.**

   After suppressing all electron-optic distortions, the minimum size of spot is only limited by light and electron-diffraction in the fluorescent screen. Curves for the allowed size of screen-particles for different number of lines in a television picture and some trial television-pictures with a resolution of 200 lines/cm are given. The limit of lines/cm depending only from electron-diffraction is calculated and confirmed experimentally resp. made visible on evaporated KCl-films. New grainless screens for small cathode ray tubes are developed.

2. **Distortionless deflection-elements for cathode ray tubes.**

   The principal electron-optical faults of deflecting coils and plates are calculated and compared with experiments. New forms of coils and plates with minimal aberrations are constructed and described, also for polar-coordinate and mechanically rotating systems. Development of new elements for compensation of trapezium and cushion distortion.

3. **Transmission of television-pictures from airplanes by a 30-W-Transmitter over 300 km.**

   Cathode-ray scanning device of small size to transmit pictures of 10 x 10 cm, wavelength 4 and 7 m. Optimal place and form of antennas, typical disturbances of synchronisation by echoes, avoidable by local synchronisations.

4. **Developments of blue-pattern cathode ray tubes.**

   Investigations about resolution, heating methods, and life of KCl-screens, especially for cathode ray tubes of high resolving power.

5. **Developments of iconoscopes.**

   Screens for different spectral-ranges, especially on Sb-Cs-base; oscillographic methods for measuring the amount of black spot and the sensitivity in different spectral ranges; diminishing of tube size; iconoscope with transparent screen and identical optical and cathode ray axis; semi-conductor screens, especially for infra-red and pick-up pictures.

6. **Developments of super-iconoscopes.**

   Supericonoscope with electrostatic lens for electron image, electrostatic deflection and screen size 2 x 2cm, with molten - on glass lens for avoiding cushion distortion; improvement of sensitivity of screens.

7. **Electron multipliers.**

   Development of different types of Sb-Cs multipliers of the grid type.

8. **Cathode ray switches.**

   First stage: Cathode ray switch with fluorescent screen and photocells.

   Second stage: Secondary emission cathode ray switches for multiple telephony on decilines, avoiding disturbances by secondary and tertiary electrons and having equal secondary emission and life for all targets.

9. **Cathode ray tubes with rectangular broken ray.**

   This tube looks like a tart-box and has a globe-condensator for constant rectangular deflection. The screen is part of a cylinder mantle, the time base a full circle, the plane of which is normal to the axis of electro-gun. The length of tube is less than 1/2 of those of a normal cathode ray tube of the same screen size; it could also be employed as cathode ray switch.

10. **Full-ceramic and full-iron cathode ray tubes.**

    Solving some problems about glass-metal and ceramic glass connections, current passages and life of cathode ray receiving tubes and switches with rectangular and level screen of 50 cm side-length.

11. **Cathode ray projection tubes.**

    Improvements of life, screen brightness and cathodes of transparent tubes up to 60 kv, of oblique angle tubes up to 80 kv. Investigations of brightness limits of such tubes, depending on heating and poisoning effects.

12. **Cathode-ray fluorescent-screen transmitting tubes.**

    Improvements of screen materials and life of such tubes.

REPORT IV

Schloss Pullach (near Bad Aibling)

This institution is a branch of the F.B.I. and is thus under the general direction of Prof. von Handel.

The scientist in charge is Dr. Pfister.

The primary object of the organisation is said to be the investigation of navigational aids using the direct, or ground wave, but other activities were noted. In addition to Prof. von Handel and Dr. Pfister, two engineers from the outstation at Irschemberg were present - Dr. Grassman and Dipl. Ing. Neun. They had worked, principally, on Erica.

The investigating party consisted of:

W/Cdr.	C.P. Edwards	R.A.F. (Team Leader)
S/Ldr.	W.E. Farvis	R.A.F.
Capt.	F. Emplin	British Army
Lt.	P.G. Redgment	R.N.V.R.

Firstly the charts for the "Erica" navigational aid system (34 mc/s, with phase meter presentation of two grids) were examined; these charts are of two types, some showing only the "Coarse" grid and others, on a larger scale, including the fine grid. Samples of both types were removed. It was stated that the phase-shifting circuits for the "Erica" system were developed by a Dr. Goldman (of Lorenz) who might be at Landshut now. As the whole accuracy of the system depends on this apparatus this should, it is considered, be followed up.

The establishment was next inspected and the following apparatus seen:-

A transmitter and Responder similar to the "Baldur" type. The apparatus had been specially designed to investigate the ultimate accuracy of range determination by Radar means, since Prof. von Handel considered that tropospheric effects would set such a limit. The apparatus was undergoing tests when work was terminated but no results had been obtained. This work may be of considerable importance in Gunnery radar. (Dr. Pfister was carrying out this work).

Some centimetric apparatus was next examined; it was understood that a little work had been carried out on jamming equipment for "Rotterdam", but it appeared to be in a very elementary state.

Centimetre propagation investigations were also envisaged and a "Corfu" receiver was available in the laboratory for this work. This receiver, it was noted, covered a band 8 cm. - 12 cm. using a magnetron type MD2 as local oscillator.

Some tunable cavity resonators stated to be for magnetrons were seen, it is possible that these were connected with the work of Dr. Kluge referred to in Part II.

The "Puck" (PS35A) test oscillator for 9 cm. equipment was also examined. It was stated that the length of the radiator determined the frequency, and other dimensions were not critical.

A complete "Bernardine" equipment was inspected; this is the receiving apparatus for use in conjunction with the "Bernard" beacon system. No "Bernard" equipment was available at Pullach but a dummy test transmitter was provided for experimental purposes.

Briefly, this system appears to use a rotating Beacon so arranged that, whilst it transmits on one R.F. channel, the amplitudes of two tones, or sub-carriers, vary in differing manners with azimuth. The two tones can be separated by filters in the receiver. One tone has one sharp zero and several subsidiary minima, whilst the other is roughly a cordioid, but with a small back lobe. The recording arrangements were made on the "Hellschreiber", and two systems are arranged in tandem on one shaft. The one is energised through filters by the cardioid diagram and this prints by Hellschreiber a part of the bearing side at the transmitter. The other prints a line, the length of which depends on signal intensity, below a certain level (saturation takes place above this). Thus a record of the signal minimum is correlated with the bearing scale at the beacon. Sample records were obtained and one is attached. The work of this establishment did not, repeat not, include the development of the system (this was actually developed by Lorenz) but an investigation into its liability to jamming was to be undertaken by Dr. Pfister.

It is considered that details of the apparatus should be investigated further.

Many documents relating to the work of this institution had been handed over previously by Prof. von Handel, but a few believed to be of interest were discovered, and removed by W/Cdr. Edwards.

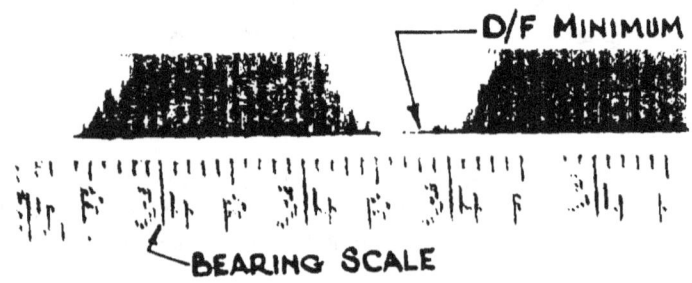

SAMPLE OF BERNADINE TAPE

PART II

Simultaneously with the investigations described above Dr. Labus and Prof. Werner Kluge were interrogated by:

    Mr. Hansell   - O.C. Sig. O.
    Capt. Snowden - British Army

Dr. Labus had, it appeared, been engaged on wavelength calculations and also theoretical investigations into the optimum proportions of cavity resonators. He had also worked on the theory of Klystrons and written a paper on the subject - this had, unfortunately, been lost during recent activities. The order of the effects obtained, however, was 10% efficiency, with a maximum power of 10 watts C.W.

Prof. Werner Kluge had been engaged on valve design in previous years, but appears to have done only the most abstract work during the war.

The major work had been on the light emitted by a crystal rectifying contact when a voltage was applied. He stated that he had observed that when the metallic electrode was positive the light was within the crystal, but on its surface with a negative electrode. All attempts to correlate this illumination with the rectifying properties had failed. It had been proposed to use the effect to provide a screen for a C.R.T. and the efficiency was such that 10 mW would give visible light.

He had also done work on cathode surfaces, both thermionic and photo. He had used an antimony/caesium alloy for image-multiplier cathodes; the effect appeared to be on the surface rather than metallic emmision.

The maximum efficiency, which occurred for monochromatic light in the blue-green region, was up to 8%, but the average over the visible spectrum was only about 0.01%.

He had also done some work on Cold Cathode Thyratrons, but did not appear to have contributed much to this subject.

Dr. Labus once worked for the General Electric Co. at Schenectady, N.Y., under the general supervision of Mr. C.A. Priest. He originally came from Prague and would like to return there.

Because of the approach of the Russians his papers and equipment were shipped from Berlin, by M. Brendel, to Burglengenfeld near Regensburg, in Bavaria addressed to Bevollmachtigter fur Hochfrequenz Forschung. He understood that all were sunk with a barge, in a canal en route, due to allied military action.

He had also written a paper which was about to be published by Hirzel of Leipzig on the subject "Enflurt der Raumladung auf der Phasenfobuss-inniz" but has no knowledge of what happened to it.

Dr. Labus' work in recent years has been concerned with theoretical calculations of cavity resonators and methods for measuring their resonant impedances. He also has made theoretical calculations and done some experimental work on electron-streams in Klystron-type tubes. He has not been concerned with any practical applications to tubes and systems actually used.

Powers of about 10 watts had been obtained from Klystrons for continuous operation. The efficiency was about 10%. Some work had been done on the pulsing of klystrons but this was chiefly theoretical.

Dr. Kluge said that during the war he had been engaged in pure research and not in any direct application work for the war. He has investigated detail phenomena observed in crystals of the general type used in radio detectors, such as carborundums with nickel-iron contact points. It has been observed that, on some areas of some of these crystals, the passage of current between the contact point and the crystal causes the crystal to give off light. When the point is positive the light comes from inside the crystal and when the point is negative it comes from the surface of the crystal. Power of about 0.01 watt has been observed to produce a visible amount of light.

He has tried to find some coordination between the production of light and the sensitivity of the crystals as radio detectors but the results have so far been inconclusive.

Dr. Kluge has also done research work on photocathodes and hot cathodes. He has experimented with light amplifiers with efficiencies of about 0.01% in the use of light in producing emission. He said that, with antimony-caesium surfaces he had obtained efficiencies as high as 8% for blue-green monochromatic light. He had also tried other elements near antimony in the periodic table, with caesium, without improved results.

The antimony-caesium surface does not saturate with increasing electric field for pulling out the emission, indicating that the emissive properties are probably due to composite surface rather than metallic emission phenomena.

He was about to attempt construction of cascade image amplifiers when his work was interrupted by the Allied invasion. He would guess, from preliminary experiments, that he might get a gain of 5 or 10 per stage for an operating voltage of 6 Kv.

In former years he seems to have been engaged in the design of commercial high-power, hot cathode, rectifier tubes and has written at least one more or less comprehensive paper on the subject, which has been published.

He has investigated phenomena of glow in low-pressure gas tubes in high-frequency electromagnetic fields and has studied effect of water-vapour in quenching ionization. According to him these things were just beginning and he had no really worth-while information to give out.

Gas discharge at Centimetre Wavelengths

By Dipl. Ing. W. Sparbier and Dipl. Ing. R. Hubner.

We were given the task of planning the construction of T.R. gaps to protect the receiver in aircraft ground-scanning radar equipment from the strong transmission pulses. This was to be done at the shortest possible wavelengths.

The technical and physical difficulties in the preparation of the gaps got greater and greater as the wavelength was shortened. Under the circumstances a point is reached at which the principle must be given up and absolutely new ways must be tried.

We therefore wish to try whether it is possible by spark induction, between antenna and receiver, to achieve a sufficient protection for the receiver so that the special spark gaps can be eliminated. It is our hope that such a principle will be easier to use, especially at the shorter wavelengths, than the present building in of special blocking elements. Our work in this difficult field is only just in progress.

In conjunction with this task we intend to investigate, experimentally the spark and striking voltage at Decimetre and Centimetre wavelengths and to work towards the clarification of the conditions for gas discharge with these waves. Our work in this field is also in progress.

Spark characteristics in gas filled three electrode tubes

By Prof. Dr. W. Kluge and Dipl. Ing. W. Sparbier.

Gas filled three electrode tubes are used in spark controlled circuits with low triggering voltages. There three electrode tubes with warm filaments are known as Thyratrons. Gas filled three electrode tubes with cold filaments are known as "Glimm relays." The two tubes are, to speak only of their most important differences, totally different in their spark characteristic, striking voltage and constancy of sparking point. The Thyratron proves so far to have the most favourable properties for technical uses, but the Glimm relay owing to its cold Cathode renders possible the construction of apparatus with less weight and less space. Whereas far reaching work has already been done on the functioning of the Thyratron, only a very little has been published about the "Glimm relay", so we undertook to study the latter. Further, we wished to improve its properties so as to compete with the Thyratron.

We were able to establish an elementary curve of the Glimm relay's characteristics, according to Fig.1. This shows the Grid voltage and the corresponding anode voltage at the moment of striking. Several easily distinguishable zones may be seen having different striking mechanisms. Leaving out subtleties, the following approximate equations for the zones are obtained.

$$A\text{-}B: \quad U_g : U_1 \approx C_1$$
$$B\text{-}C: \quad U_g + D_A U_A = U_2 \approx C_2$$
$$C\text{-}D: \quad U_A \approx C_3$$
$$D\text{-}E: \quad U_A (1 + DK) - U_g = U_4 \approx C_4$$
$$E\text{-}F: \quad U_A - U_g = U_5 \approx C_5$$
$$F\text{-}G: \quad -U_g = U_6 \approx C_6$$

in which C_1 to C_6 are constants. DA and DK are the intersection the Anode and Cathode with the stretch formed by the two other electrodes (?). In production tubes, parts of this characteristic curve are always suppressed so that it looks different for every tube. Certain parts of the characteristic are, on account of their striking mechanism, especially well adapted to induction striking with small control voltages. The investigation of this zone of the characteristic forms part of our work on the tubes. In this connection we are striving to clarify the striking current ratios in all zones.

For comparison with the Glimm relay's characteristic, a Thyratron characteristic has also been included in figure 1. The amount of voltage required to work the Thyratron (after striking) is of the order of its Ionisation voltage, but essentially higher in the case of the Glimm relay. In this way one can distinguish whether Glimm striking is preferable to Spark striking.

We tried whether we could get a Glimm relay with a characteristic approximating the technically more favourable one of the Thyratron. In figure 2 may be seen how, by the introduction of charge carriers into a Glimm relay, the striking characteristic is displaced from right to left by stepping up the number of charge carriers introduced from outside. (Connected line = Glimm relay characteristic, dotted line Thyratron characteristic). It is not possible to obtain a continuous characteristic of the Thyratron type but under certain conditions in which a discharge of higher voltage

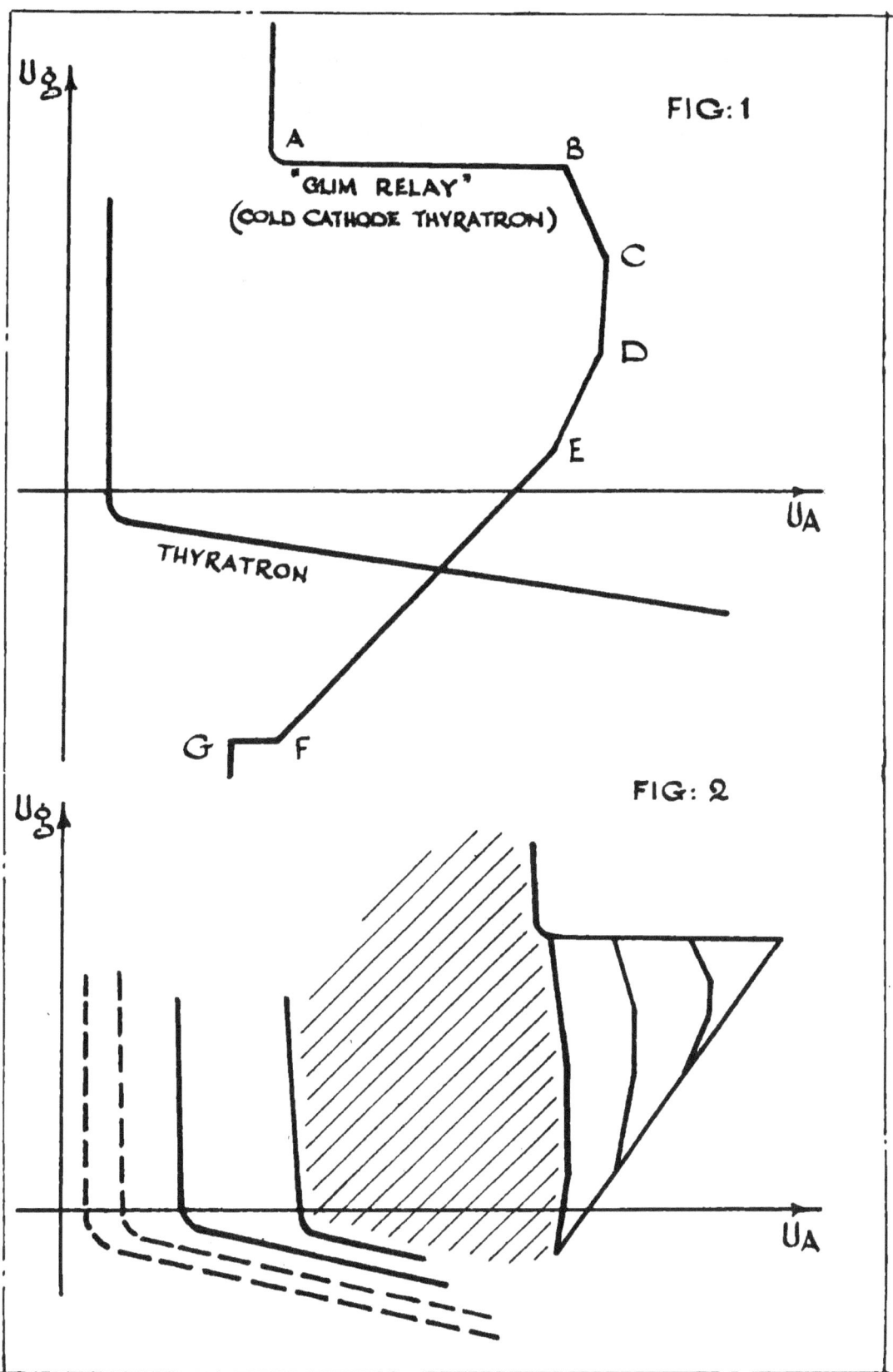

than a Glimm discharge is set up, a striking characteristic of Thyratron nature may be established. In principle it is a matter of indifference whether the charge carriers are brought in by beaming, auxiliary discharge or glow emission. (In the shaded zone no sharp striking took place).

To avoid outside influence in the production of the charge carriers introduced, we paid especial heed to the radiation of the striking zone by the appropriate inclusion of a radio active substance. In our experiments we brought the radiating substance on to a ring shaped part of the electrode surrounding the discharge zone. We are trying to see whether it is physically possible to reach a Glimm relay characteristic of Thyratron nature with technically practicable media.

Besides the attempted displacement of the characteristic, we expect a total improvement of the striking point constant as opposed to un-radiated Glimm relays. A good constancy of striking point would itself be a valuable advance, even if the displacement of the characteristic can't be achieved.

We believe we have solved the problem of introducing the radio-active substance into the tube system by vacuum technique free from objections and capable of production.

Gases with high ionisation potential are indicated for a favourable use of radio active radiation. It is yet to be seen whether they should be used in a pure state or with addition to others, or whether the usual gas mixtures for Glimm relay can be adhered to.

The "Bildwandler" as a "Light Amplifier"
by Prof. W. Kluge

It is known that an optical image thrown on a photo-cathode can be changed into a latent electron image and that this can be made visible again by electron bombardment of a fluorescent screen. If infra-red photo cathodes with the structure $Ag-Cs_2O-Cs$ and infra-red light are used to produce the light-optical image, then invisible images can be made visible (Bildwandler). Especially sharp images are obtained if an electronic-optical lens is inserted between the photo-cathode and the fluorescent screen. cf. Fig. 1

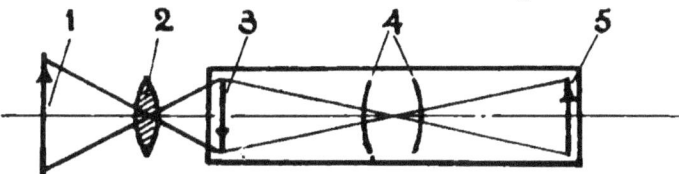

1. OBJECT 2. OBJECTIVE 3. PHOTOCATHODE 4. ELECTROSTATIC LENS
5. FLUORESCENT SCREEN

FIG: 1

The light strength of the electronic optical image increases somewhat exponentially with increasing voltage. In practice however it has been found that the voltage can scarcely be raised above 18-20 kv. New complications set in, e.g. destruction of the photo cathode surface by bombardment by positive ions, etc. In order to transform weak light-optical images into strong electronic-optical images, that is to "amplify" them, an attempt must accordingly be made to improve the sensitivity of the photo-cathode and of the light screen.

We have succeeded in making a photo-cathode, first constructed by Gorlich, especially sensitive to passage of light. Transparency is necessary for the further development of the light amplifier, as is shown below. The transparent layers are composed of Antimony and Caesium (Sb-Cs). It is still an open question whether this is an alloy or a chemical compound (Metalloid). Our experiments and measurements gave for such layers in yellow-green light (selective maximum) a quantum gain of 8-10%. In contrast, up to the present in all other photo-cathodes known so far, at best values of only .1 to .5% were obtained in the selective maximum. The saturation currents of Sb-Cs cathodes lie between 30-60 microA/Lumen. We presume that the sensitivity of such photo-cathodes can be increased still further, if the conditions of preparation are varied. Finally we assume that there are other chemical elements beside Antimony that can become very effective light-electrically in combination with Caesium.

Now we built the above described sensitive Sb-Cs photo-cathode into a simple image-changer tube which also had no other electrical lens. Light amplification factors were then measured at a voltage of 10 kv and gave a set of figures between 6 & 8. Zinc sulphide with a very small refraction was used as a light-screening substance.

The amplification of the light can be pushed even further by connecting two image-changer tubes, one behind the other. The mere interposition of two separated tubes in the intermediate stages by an objective brings little gain however. Consequently we busied ourselves with this difficult question and think we have found a workable solution (Fig.2).

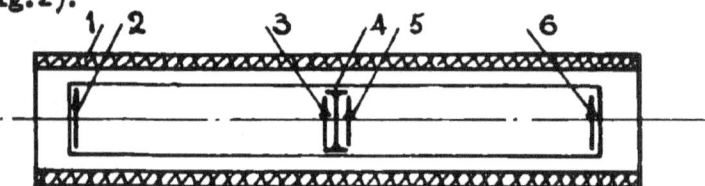

1. LONG LENS 2 & 5. PHOTOCATHODES 3 & 6 FLUORESCENT SCREENS
4. GLASS FOIL   FIG: 2

A very thin smooth foil of glass is set in the middle of an image-changing tube. The one side of this foil is now furnished with a sensitive fluorescent screen, the other with a sensitive photo-cathode. Then the first electronic-optical image can be "copied" onto a second photo-cathode through the glass foil. At the present stage of our work we can prepare sheets of about 3-4 cm. diameter with a thickness of .01 mm. The building of such foils into image-changing tubes has never before been attempted. But the small thickness of the foil will make it possible to avoid reducing appreciably the definition of the 2nd image as compared with the 1st. Moreover, it is possible to make the sheets optically plane and taut. Both, sheet and coating, are formed in one mass, so that the danger of shaking can also be ignored.

We also believe we shall succeed in getting effective amplification of light in the way described. Perhaps it is then possible to make visual observations on light which lies below the threshold of visibility of the human eye. The significance of the light-amplifier in the field of telescopy may be briefly mentioned.

(a) Glow-cathodes heated by burning

(b) Heat-retaining Cathode construction
    by Prof. W. Kluge and Dipl. Ing. Sparbier

(a) It is often necessary to use once and for a short time glow-cathode tubes, high vacuum and gas filled tubes. In such cases it is mainly required to have them as small and light as possible. In this connection we have experimented in the development of indirectly heated glow-cathodes which acquire no heat energy from outside during their functioning; in which therefore sources of heat can be dispensed with.

We have introduced a construction in which instead of the usual method of heating, a heater element is inserted into the inside of the little cathode tube and burns during the time the tube works and thus provides the cathode with the necessary emission temperature. To protect the discharge chamber from pollution by the heater, the inside of the little cathode tube must be hermetically sealed from it. The heater can only be fitted in after the manufacture of the cathode, the combustion chamber must remain in connection with the outer air. Therefore we are compelled to use a method of construction such as is shown.

A small tube, open at one end, stands in the middle of the discharge container and is hermetically connected on its open side with the tube envelope. The heater is inside the little tube whose surface is covered with the emission layer. The electrodes are connected to the cathode in the usual ways. One can imagine a construction using little tubes open on both sides, but excessively high requirements of material arise owing to the heating of the little tube. All the experimental tubes we made in this way burst.

The heater can be kindled by electrical current pulses. The energy for this can be supplied by an auxiliary apparatus, which has nothing further to do with the operation and can be used as often as you please. We worked two different kinds of heater. An element can be selected which burns out very slowly and always keeps only a part of the cathode at the required temperature, or one which burns out quickly, and glows for a very long time. In the first kind we have obtained combustion times up to two minutes, with the second up to about 50 secs. Those used by us are related to Thermite. We hope by the further development of the elements of the appropriate construction with hot, quickly burning elements and colder, slowly burning ones, to reach an even duration of temperature and a raising of the time of operation. Especially long operation times may be expected from rod-formed tube construction with slow burning elements. Up to the present we have only measured temperatures; measurements of emission are still outstanding. Vacuum tight tubes of the given kind having the necessary heating requirements have been prepared in one laboratory using metal-glass construction and ceramic glass construction. We hope to make improvements by collaboration with Ceramics firms. We wish to collaborate with producer firms for the further development of heating elements.

(b) With the same construction another principle of working can be applied. Instead of the burning element, a heat conducting rod, preferably of Silit (Siemens-Plania) is introduced into the little tube. If this be heated from an auxiliary source of heat current not directly belonging to the apparatus before the actual operation time the cathode can be kept for a longer time at the emission temperature even after the heating current has been switched off, owing to the heat-retaining property of the massive cathode construction. Our experiments in this sense are only in the early stages. We are hoping for good results with a short-time heating of the rod above the temperature of emission so that a stronger fall of temperature between the inside of the cathode and the surface plate held at emission temperature results.

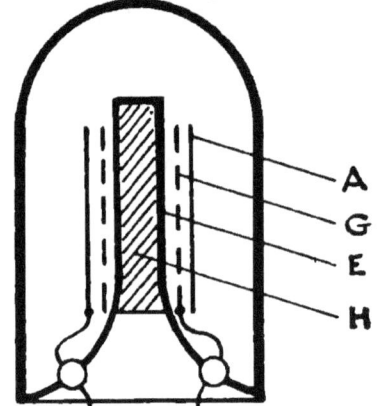

A. ANODE
G. GRID
E. EMISSIVE SURFACE
H. HEATER

FIG: 1.

On the Contact-lighting of Carborundum Crystals

Here follows a report on a lighting effect by carborundum detectors which was originally discovered some time ago (1924?) by Claus in Halle. This effect has in our opinion received too little attention since then and appears to us to be of far reaching consequence in the investigation of the principles of detection.

Common commercial Carborundum, as used in electric arcs is used, so it is not a question of pure colorless SiC. The material contains many more metallic admixtures of various kinds brought about by the production process and which lead to the coloring - green, blue or black. If fragments of the Carborundum are brought into connection with a metal contact (steel, nickel) - see fig.1 - a lighting phenomenon is observed in the vicinity of the contact.

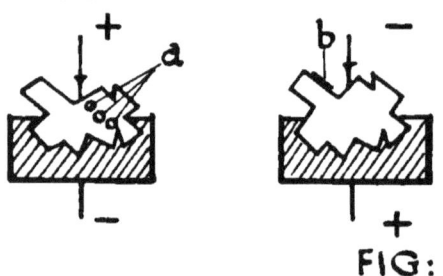

a. POINTS OF BLUISH LIGHT
b. SUPERFICIAL YELLOW LIGHT

FIG: 1.

If the metallic contact is chosen positive; then a bluish light results which is located in the depth of the crystal and consists of one or several points, also chains of points. With negative metallic points however, a yellow superficial light is produced directly on the outer surface of the crystal. In the most favourable circumstances, the light can be observed by the human eye at a voltage of only about 8-10 volts, and about 1 mA. As the electrical energy brought in is increased, the lighting increases in intensity and range till finally the place of contact glows owing to the heating. This lighting phenomenon does not arise at all points of contact; rather, suitable spots have to be looked for. Fresh lines of fracture are, as a rule, less suitable.

We asked ourselves the question: What is the explanation of this effect? We do not believe in a light excitation by a slowing up of the electrons. Also a glowing gas discharge between the crystal and the metal contact cannot take place, for the phenomenon also arises when the detector is arranged in a vacuum. Nor is it a temperature glowing, for the light effect is instantaneous and can also be produced in the open air. If the metallic points are replaced by a superficial conducting electrode (electrolyte), light phenomena are equally observed(!). Finally it is interesting that the carborundum crystal can be excited to fluorescence by radiation from ultra-violet rays. It can be frozen in the open air. The resulting light is comparable in color with the contact light described above.

For all these reasons, we believe that in the experimental arrangement shown in fig. 1 we are dealing with a phenomenon of luminosity. This luminosity is apparently due to the metallic mixtures which act as activators in the SiC grid.

On all these grounds, we are planning to prepare synthetic SiC crystals with activators in specific quantities. We wish further to investigate the connection between the rectifying operation and the lighting phenomenon. Perhaps these connections may help to throw light on the operation of detectors and so have a fruitful influence on the development of high frequency detectors too.

REPORT V

Ferdinand Braun Institute. Outstation at Gaisberg

Date May 28th, 1945

Investigators:
- W/C. Edwards,   R.A.E.
- S/L. Farvis,   T.R.E.
- Lt. Redgment,   A.S.E.
- Capt. Caplin,   S.R.D.E.
- Mr. Omberg,   U.S.Sigs.Corps.

Personnel Interviewed

Prof. von Handel
Dr. Hahnel

Dr. Hahnel is in charge of the station. His assistant scientific staff are Dr. Jakob and Dipl. Ing. Engelbrecht. His total staff numbers 15. The projects on which this station has been engaged are listed below.

1. Propagation measurements

10 cm centimetric tropospheric propagation experiments have been carried on in conjunction with Dr. Pfister. No important contributions to date.

2. Detection of Shell bursts

Dr. Hahnel was working on the detection by centimetre radar of the blast wave and hot gases following the explosion of a shell. The equipment is almost ready for the tests, and consists of a Rotterdam equipment mounted on a 70 ft. tower, in a Wurzburg mirror, to give the greatest possible gain and resolution. A suitable hill-top for practice shell bursts lies 2 km away. To make quantitative measurements of the returns from the dense gases a "standard" of reflection has been set up on a very large rock at a distance of about 1 km.

3. Communications

The station was originally one of the terminal and relay stations in an extensive 50 cm F.M. multi-channel communication-link system. The American Signal Corps wants to make use of the system, and Dr. Hahnel's engineers are doing some of the repair work on the terminal equipment. There are several DMG 5k (Michael) and also DMG 3aG (Rudolf) sets. As these have already been described fully in allied technical intelligence literature no details need be given here.

Jamming of H2S The jammer employed was a tunable 10 watt magnetron RD2Me modulated with 100 kc/s sine wave. A slow mechanical frequency wobble was provided to allow for errors in setting on frequency. Monitoring was by means of a standard Korfu receiver (E351) for 8-12 cm, made by Blaupunkt. The name of this H2S jammer was Roderich. Full details of results obtained during the experiments are given in captured C.I.O.S. documents. Roderich is made by Siemens.

Future work The projects on which experiments were shortly to commence were

1. modulation of corner reflectors to give aerodrome recognition for Rotterdam aircraft.

2. preparation of radar prediction maps.

Laboratories The laboratories are in good condition and well stocked. A sensitivity measuring equipment for the 10 cm band employing the noise diode LG 16 as a standard noise level was examined. It appears that this is the standard way of measuring sensitivity.

Documents

The following documents were collected from Dr. Hahnel:

1. Ruckstrahlbilder bei 9 cm und 150 cm Wellenlange
   (C.I.O.S. Munchen Ref: IVA/1106)

2. Vorschlag zur Direkten Storung von Bodenbetrachtungsgeraten mittels Impulssendern
   (C.I.O.S. Munchen Ref: IVE/152)

3. Untersuchungen uber die Storung von Bodenbetrachtungsgeraten
   (C.I.O.S. Munchen Ref: IVE/153)

4. Die Storung Bodenbetrachtungsgeraten durch da zu synchron laufende Impulssender
   (C.I.O.S. Munchen Ref: IVE/154)

5. Vorversuche zur Frage der indirekten Storung von Bodenbetrachtungsgeraten.
   (C.I.O.S. Munchen Ref: IVE/155)

S/Ldr. Farvis

REPORT VI

Ferdinand Braun Institute. Outstation Irschenberg

Date May 25th 1945

Investigators
W/C. Edwards	R.A.E.	
S/L. Farvis	T.R.E.	CIOS Group 1
Lt. Redgment	A.S.E.	
Capt. Caplin	S.R.D.E.	

Personnel Interviewed

Prof. von Handel
Dr. Gassmann
Dipl. Ing. Neun
Dr. Lehfeldt (Siemens)

The principal interest at this outstation, which stands on very high ground overlooking a wide plain, was the complete Erika installation. The number of the station is Erika 3: Nos. 1 and 2 were at Boulogne and Cherbourg respectively and have been destroyed as has also number 4 which was outside Wien. Stations 3 and 4 between them gave coverage of the greater part of Germany.

The Erika uses 6 identical aerial systems 3 long, each fed by a 5 kw transmitter. The arrangement of the aerials on each of the six towers is as shown.

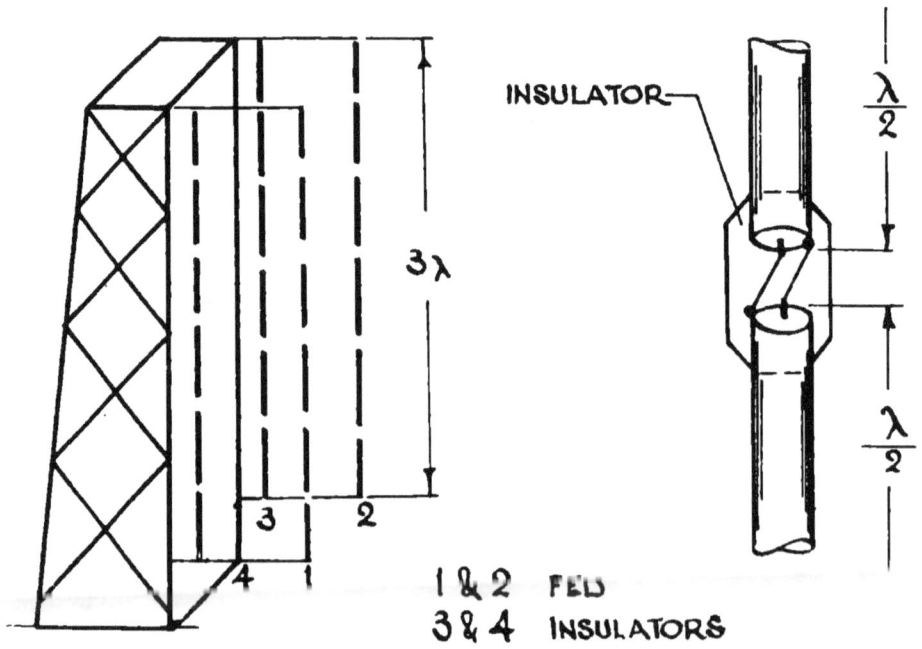

1 & 2 FED
3 & 4 INSULATORS

(1) and (2) are driven end-fed half-wave dipoles, with (3) and (4) as tuned parasitic reflectors.

The method of feeding the dipoles is as shown. This method allows hot air to be blown through the aerials in icing weather, and also gives drainage for condensation water.

All transmitters and control gear are in perfect working order. There is also a complete set of airborne equipment at the station.

The station was used in conjunction with Wien for experimental and training purposes.

The laboratories contained standard test equipment of good quality in a wide range.

An evacuee to the station was Dr. Lehfeldt of Siemens and Halske who had recently come down from Berlin. He was engaged on centimetre propagation experiments and was building new equipment at Irschenberg which would provide him with the necessary test transmitters and receivers for 10 cm and 3 cm. A Tunis equipment was available for the receiving end. Although his equipment in the North had been completed and set up on the Baltic Coast, no results were obtained before he had to leave. A short statement of his earlier work is included in this report.

The tube which Dr. Lehfeldt is using for 10 cm transmission is the LD 90, a high voltage (2 Kv) lighthouse concentric-line type of triode developed by Dr. Steimel of Telefunken. It is understood that CIOS teams 12th Army Group have full details of this tube, and of its predecessors LD 9 and LD 7. When blown the LD 90 will give 10 watts output at 10 cm.

An interesting point in connection with the tube LD 90 is that it was incorporated in a jammer called Feuermolch developed by Lorentz and Siemens to jam H2S from the ground. No details of the jammer were known, apart from the fact that it had to be used in conjunction with the Korfu 8-12 cm warning receiver and that a horn antenna was used. A dielectric antenna for 3 cm was being developed, he understood. Between 50 and 100 models have been completed and he thought were in use.

Documents

Documents removed either at the time of this interrogation, or subsequently by other Group 1 members.

1. Complete set of "Gross" line charts for Erika 3 and 4 area.

2. 3 copies of one chart giving "Fein" lines.

3. Paper by Dr. Lehfeldt "Researches about the propagation of U.S.W. upon optical lines" - attached.

4. Complete circuit diagrams and other documents appropriate to the running of the station.

Recommendations

1. That the station should be left intact, with its engineers, so that trials can be conducted.

2. That the circuit diagrams etc. referred to in 4 above should be sent to R.A.E. for safe custody.

                                                          W.E.J. Farvis   S/L.

Researches about the propagation of ultra-short waves over optical paths

By Dr. Lehfeldt, laboratory of Siement u. Halske.
Institute of Radio Research, Irschenberg

While the propagation of the short waves (λ = 10 to 100 mtrs.) is characteristically influenced by the Ionosphere, it is the refractive index of the troposphere which causes irregularities on the propagation of ultra short waves (λ = 10 mtrs.).

We have explored in detail the propagation of the waves between 0.6 and 6 mtrs on a number of lines over land with and without optical sight. Last time measures over sea had commenced, but our stations at Rugen, Bornholm and Misdroy are occupied now by the Russian army.

Our measures represent records over several years. Sound-frequency-modulated transmitters are received over distances of 30 to 200 miles and the detected sounds are recorded as measure for the high-frequency amplitude.

The constancy over long time of the transmitting power and of amplification and linearity of the receivers were ensured by particular tricks.

About the results of the measurements we notice here shortly:

(1) Statistical material about the usefulness of radio paths in the named wave-band, in dependence of time of day or time of year and of the geographical situation, i.e. probability of the appearance of fadings in differential great.

(2) Dependence of fadings from wave lengths and situation of the receivers.

(3) Diminution and removal of fading by use of multiple receiving.

(4) Increase of disturbances with increasing frequency; the absence of fading on waves of 6 mtrs length on optical paths.

(5) "Hyperextension", i.e. receiving far beyond the optical horizon only by weather, which adds the appearance of fadings with the optical horizon.

Theoretical considerations about the influence of the refractive index in the troposphere particularly on diffuse boundaries or layers, in which the refractive index strongly varies, makes clear the results of measurements.

As far as is known in Germany, theory and results of measurement agree also with publications of American workers from the years until 1942. But they exceed extraordinary the material, which is published till now in German or in English. Especially we believe, that nowhere are made such systematical measures on many paths and on different wave-lengths on the same path.

The measurements over sea must be continued in the same manner of measurement. Furthermore preparations are nearly finished to make similar measures with waves down to 9 cm and eventually yet shorter.

Institute of Radio Research
Station "Erika" near Irschenberg

The station "Erika" review for information.

The station "Erika" belongs to the Institute of Radio Research Brannenburg/Inn. Competent to all questions is the director of the Institute of Radio Research Prof. Dr. Ing. Paul Freiherr von Handel, who already has had transactions with officers of 12th Armd. Div. U.S.A.

The station firstly was in service for trying the "Erika" fine navigation method, whose inventor is Dr. Pfister of our institute. Moreover the Station was used especially to research the propagation of ultrashort waves. There are six transmitters of ultrashort waves (each has a power of 5 Kw) and four receiver stations for measuring and controlling: two stations in distance of ca 3 km near Mangfall, one station north of Munchen and one incomplete station in the Fichtel Mountains.

The documents of our recent inquiries we have brought in security to several places in the neighbourhood, because we feared that they would be destroyed by bomber action. All published accounts including the secret ones you may see at Dr. Pfister in Pullach near Bad-Aibling or at the Directory of our institute in Brannenburg/Inn.

Signed by Dr. Gabmann.

Addresses:

Directory of Institute of Radio Research: Brannenburg/Inn. Prof. Dr. Ing. Freiherr von Telefon Brannenburg Nr.64.

Chief of department 1: Dr. Pfister, Castle pullach near Bad-Aibling, Telephone Aibling Nr. 286.

Station "Erika" near Irschenberg: Dr. Gabmann, Telephon Bruckmuhl Nr.3.

The Erika "Fine-Navigation" method

In an airplane are placed two kinds of watches, the hands of which show two numbers of coordinates in space, coming from two transmitter-stations like two crossing fans. In comparison with a map, where the beams of the two fans are drawn and numbered, the pilot is able to see the position of his airplane at any moment.

The method was developed as a result of research on the propagation of ultra-short waves. The principle is the measurement of phase difference between two tones of 50 cs received in the airplane as modulations of two high-frequency waves about 9 m wavelength transmitted by Erika-stations. These two tones drive two synchronized motors in the watch. The two motors are coupled with one another by a "Differential" (known from the motor car). Each change of phase difference of the tones is shown by a turning of the hand.

The construction of the station is made in such a way that there are six antennas mounted at six different towers, two antennas of which form a unit, so that we have 3 pairs of antennas. The distances of each pair of antennas are strictly defined (2, 3 and 27λ). These three pairs of antennas transmit three different high frequency waves modulated with a tone of ca 50 cs. There is a special way of modulation in making the high frequency of one antenna of the pair about 50 cs higher than the other by a motor-driven phase-shifter known as "goniometer" of special construction. The three modulated frequencies are destined for three systems called (translated) "rough", "relation" and "Fine" (in relation to the above defined distances of antennas).

The afore-mentioned motors in the watches of airplane now are driven in such a way that the first motor goes with the tone "relation" and the second one with "rough" or "fine". By changing the wavelength from "rough" to "fine" the pilot can see his position line to the exactness of the "fine" system, thirty times as accurate as the rough system.

It will be clear that the phases of the two tones are functions of the position of the airplane in open space. It would be easier to understand the functions by thinking of only one tower for the system "relation", the high frequency of which is amplitude-modulated with 50 cs. That tone would be the fixed point for the phase measuring. There were practical causes to make all the three systems alike. In the before-mentioned case the distances of antennas for "fine" and "rough" would have been $27 + 3$, 30λ and $3 - 2 = 1\lambda$. That is the cause why the distance of 27 instead of 30λ has been chosen.

These explanations must be sufficient for the complicated theory of phase measuring by "Erika".

As was explained, we have two transmitter stations for position-finding. In practice, the pilot receives with the wavelength for "rough" and after having reached his target measures with "fine". He has to receive 6 wavelengths. For each watch he receives at first the rough.

The exactness of the measuring should be $\pm$ 600 feet at a range from airplane to transmitter of 300 miles. We had two stations in Germany, one near Munich and the other near Vienna. The station near Vienna can be reached, but it could only transmit for short times because of minor faults in construction of sets. On account of the simplicity of service the method has become especially useful for peace and there is no doubt that it would be the best of all kinds of navigation methods.

We have considered simplifying the apparatus recently, by using four high-frequency receivers with two additional amplifiers and two watches, but these projects had to be stopped by other tasks for war.

                                              Diplom. Ingenieur Neun
                                                Station Erika.

REPORT VII

Investigation of Komet Experimental Site at Ismaning
(Adjacent to Radio Munich)

Date 21 May 1945

Investigators W/C Edwards, R.A.E.
Mr. Soderman, A.B.L.15   } CIOS Group 1
S/L. Farvis, T.R.E.

Personnel Interrogated: Dr. Streimer, BHF
Dr. Scherzer, BHF
Dr. Birkheim, Ferdinand Braun Inst.

Dr. Birkheim was the engineer engaged on the experimental work for Prof. von Handel (Ferdinand Braun Inst.). Dr. Streimer and Dr. Scherzer belong to a different organisation but are evacuated from Berlin and live on the same site.

Komet is a long range navigational aid for use by aircraft or ships: the Luftwaffe were the sponsors for the research project in the first instance, but the Kriegsmarine later became interested and proceeded to conduct their own experiments at Sonderburg in Denmark on a modified system called Wollenwever, assisted by ENK (Dr. Bachem), Konstanz.

There have been 2 forms of Komet, providing different methods of eliminating (or allowing for) the azimuthal error due to the angle of elevation of the sky wave on which observation is made. No such error is obtained if the equi-signal plane is normal to the aerial array, and the first Komet system used large numbers of aerials $3°$ apart. A pair of aerials could then be chosen which gave an equisignal in approx. the required direction, and normal to the line joining the pair of aerials. The aerials for one frequency range were thus arrayed around the arc of a circle and several sets of aerials (of different heights) were arrayed concentrically so that a number of frequencies would be available for different times of day.

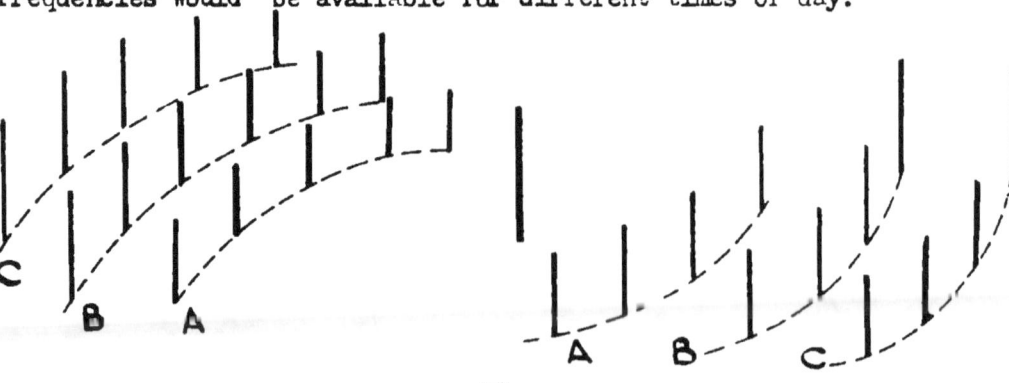

Such a Komet system was installed at Bordeaux and was captured by the Allies, but no equipment had been installed. As far as these personnel are informed, no other site had been installed with this type. Considerable technical difficulty was experienced in feeding the aerials due to the coupling between the elements of such a complicated network. The difficulties were never solved and the system was dropped.

It was succeeded by the much simplified 5-aerial system which was inspected at this target. Two "basic-lines" only are used A_2 B_2 & A_1, B_1.

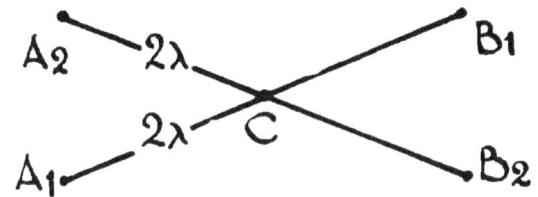

At Ismaning the angle between the arrays is 30°: this is not critical and is chosen by consideration of the area to be covered by the system.

C is a central omni-directional aerial.

The phases of the currents in A_2, B_2 were rotated by means of a goniometer which is driven mechanically at a slow speed:-

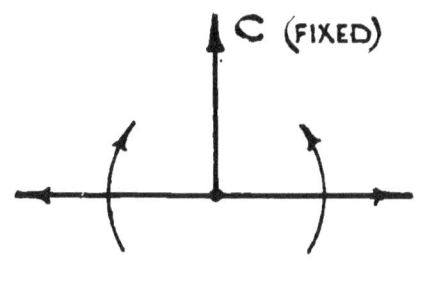

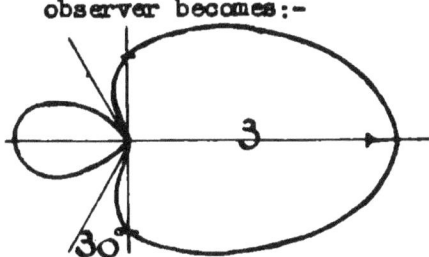

Tracing out the field strength at a remote point over one cycle of events the resultant "polar diagram" at the observer becomes:-

The complete rotation of A_2 & B_2 phases takes 6 seconds approximately, i.e. the beacon apparently rotates through the observer in 6 secs.

In addition to this slow phase rotation by the goniometer A_2 & B_2 are each changed 180° in phase at a switching rate of 70 per second:-

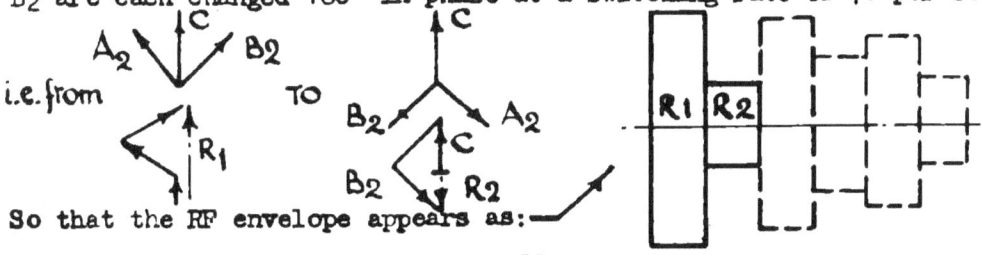

i.e. from   TO

So that the RF envelope appears as:—

For monitoring purposes these envelopes are observed by filling in with a 1000 cps beat note in the receiving equipment. On a slow time base the IF envelope appears as below (a picture which has been photographed many times in England):-

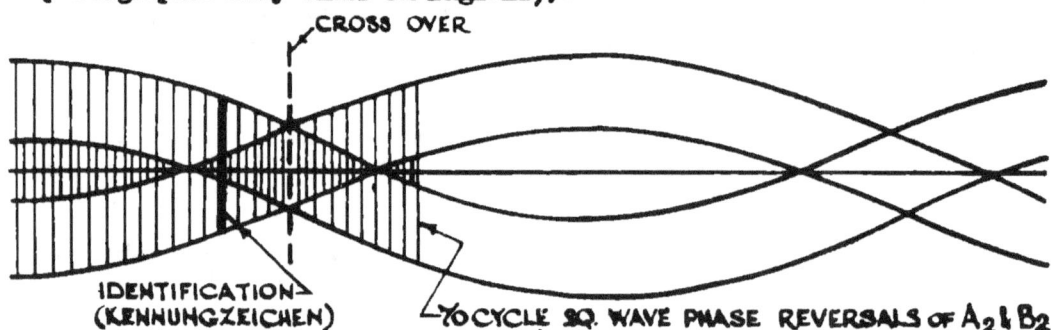

A short break (Kennungzeichen) is made in the transmission to provide a reference bearing.

At the transmitting station, monitoring of the phasing and "Kennungzeichen" is obtained by means of remote receivers mounted on a circular arc at a distance of approximately 200 meters, and the outputs of which are brought to the control desk. The receivers can be selected at will.

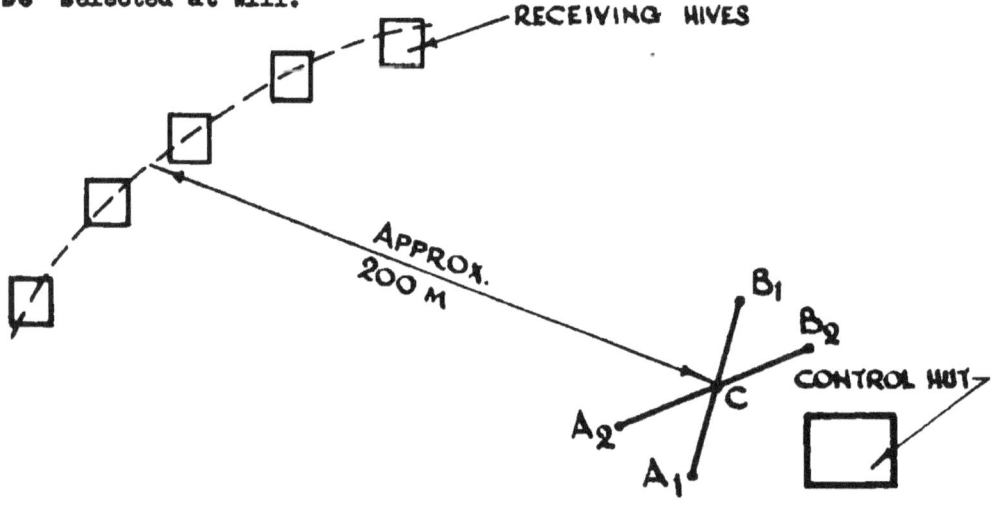

At the receiving station the bearing of the beacon is obtained from a measurement of the time interval between the characteristic break in the transmission, and the cross-over point.

Errors due to angle of elevation

The time interval between the pip and the cross-over enables the bearing of the beacon from the observer to be found. However, timing between the observed cross-over and the break only gives the true azimuth angle, when the observer is on a line perpendicular to the array. At any other azimuth angle, and owing to the angle of elevation of the sky wave on which observation is made, the observed angle is in error owing to the unequal distances from the outer aerials. The equisignal surface is in fact not a plane but a hyperboloid.

In order that this convenient type of rotating beacon can be used with a high degree of accuracy the elevation-angle-distortion is allowed for by having a second complete aerial system whose base line is inclined at some arbitrary angle to that of the first system (e.g. $A_1 CB_1$ inclined to $A_2 CB_2$ at approximately $30°$ at Munich). True azimuth angle is given from the projection on the ground of the point of intersection of the two hyperboloids from system 1 and system 2 respectively, and is found from a chart.

Measuring the Time Intervals

Determination of the time intervals from Kennungzeichen to crossover for system 1 and system 2 is done from an automatic recorder fitted in the aircraft or ship. The record appears as below.

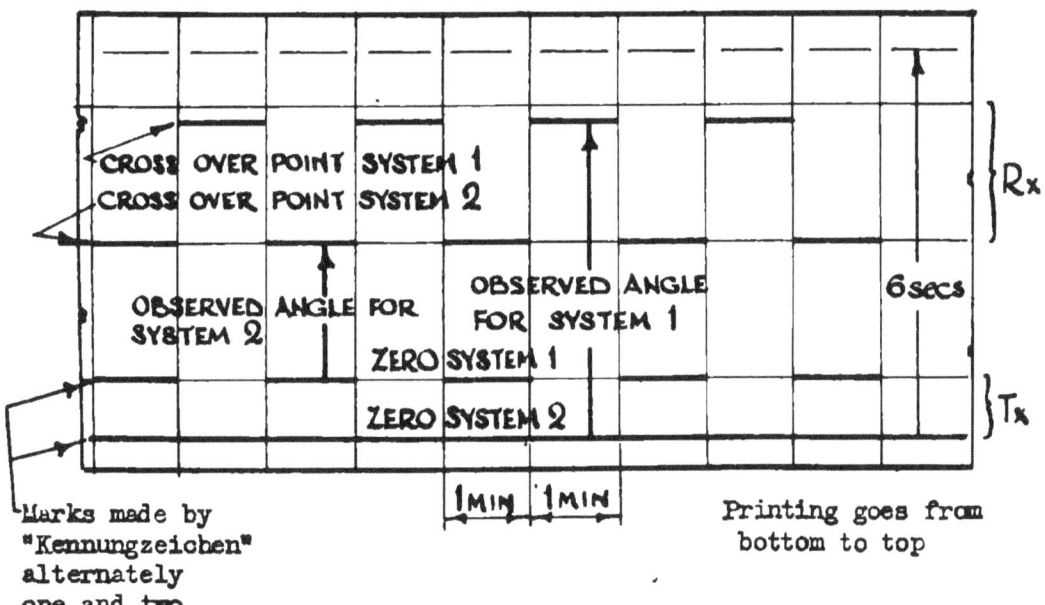

Marks made by "Kennungzeichen" alternately one and two

Printing goes from bottom to top

Recorder Mechanism

A simple single-thread spline-type recording drum rotates once in 6 seconds, continuously-driven in synchronism with the goniometer.

The spline is inked and normally the paper, which is fed past it at a rate of approximately one centimetre per minute, is not in contact with the spline.

The rocker frame which holds it away from the spline is pivoted and is connected to a relay armature so that the paper touches the drum whenever the relay is operated.

The relay is arranged to operate whenever the 70 cycle component vanishes, i.e. at each break and at the cross-over points. In this way, the record illustrated above is produced.

Performance

It is claimed that by using the correct frequency (from a table provided by Dr. Dieminger of the ionospheric forecasting service an accuracy of $0.7°$ is possible and the maximum error observed on the Berlin - Sicily line was $1.5°$ throughout the seasons. (This line was normal to the line joining the aerials and so only one system was used, sending 2 breaks continuously).

Ranges of 1000 to 1500 km are claimed.

No operational trials have ever been made.

The time taken to obtain a fix, using two Komet stations, is 4 minutes minimum, and may in practice take up to 10 minutes.

Frequencies so far employed have been

5.13 Mc/s   6.75 Mc/s   9.83 Mc/s

Transmitter power was 800 watts

Documents

No documents were available at the Komet site but a good description of the background work is given in a general report by the Ferdinand Braun Institute called:-

    Beitrage fur Theorie u. Technik der Funknavigation
    Teil 1 (Nv 802/1)
    Teil 2 (Nv 802/2)

Sequence

Aerial system 1 is operated for one minute with only one "Kennungzeichen" break then the change-over is made to aerial system 2 for the next minute, identification being given by the presence of 2 "Kennungzeichen" and so on with alternate minutes of the transmission being from system 1 and then system 2.

REPORT VIII

Swifting, near Sandsberg/Lech. Part of Sky-wave Section

Investigated by:	C.P. Edwards	W/C R.A.E.
	F. Caplin	Capt. S.R.D.E.
	Omberg	O.C.Sig O.

Date: 26 May 1945

Location: Swifting village 5 km E of Sandsberg. Wooden building under guard.

Dispersal Stores:
Unterschondorf on Ammer See. Lab. instruments of good quality, HF and VHF. House of Ludgig Weigh, 138 Schondorf.
Epfenhausen 7 km NE of Sandsberg. Raw materials, screws, etc.
Airfield Sandsberg. HF cable: transmitter parts for Komet.
" " SW side: junk store and 6 mast Adcock station.
School house Swifting. Bulk now returned to laboratories.

Personnel: Ten qualified staff in total complement of about 40.

(1) Dr. Crone (Abteilungslieter: Raumweller) formerly on X-ray work Zenneck at Munich.
Performance measurements on Electra, Komet and other HF CW navigational systems.

(2) Dr. Martin formerly with Debye on molecular physics.
Carried out experiments on under direction of Graf Soden von Frauenhofenon the Frequency modulation of pulses to increase range of radar equipment. Work incomplete. <u>Soden's</u> name appears on an office at Brannenburg, but he is thought to be either in Munich or at his castle near Landshut.

(3) Dr. Mitzaika, formerly on cosmic ray research.
Investigation of ionospheric propagation in relation to solar phenomena. Recently working on centimetre-wave telephony and beaconry using gas tube modulators associated with Prof. Knoll in this work.

(4) Dipl. Phys. Dessauer, formerly under Zenneck.
Worked at Kochel and later at Swifting on propagation measurements for sky-wave nav. systems.

Also worked with Crone on the discharge of aircraft static by addition of dibromethylene (0.85%) to the fuel. Jet propelled aircraft were used. A report which may be very important was collected, entitled "Elektrostatische Einaufladungen von Flugzeugen und ein neuer weg zu deren Beseitigung" von G.Dessauer of 1.2.1944.

(5) Dr.Friedl, formerly under Beck at Tubigen University. Head of experimental group at Ismanning station. At Swifting, Friedl also worked on anti-interference radar by F.M. pulses.

(6) Dipl. Ing. Hummrich, formerly TH Darnstadt, on electron optics.

(7) Dipl. Ing. Sandstorfer

(8) Herr Strack. ex-Telefunken. Adcock D/F specialist.

(9) Herr Weber. Teacher. Statistical expert who analysed records.

(10) Dr. Zimmerman. Student of Barkhausen at Dresden.

Documents

Many documents remain at Swifting, the large majority being records of Komet navigation system measurements, the main work of this laboratory.
The following reports not generally issued by F.B.Inst. were extracted:-

(1) "Arbeiten der Abt. 3 des Ferdinand-Braun - Institutes, Swifting 13.5.45." It is a complete statement and contains much important detail.

(2) A report on discharge of aircraft static referred to under Dessauer.

(3) Results of propagation measurements on the Komet system over a long period. No yet issued but copies are being prepared at Swifting for collection on or about 1st June 1945.

(4) Two copies of chart for determination of 2 & B from the known values of S_1 & S_2 (Komet System).

    N.B. The remaining technical data on Komet is available among the official reports of the F.B. Institutes, and a complete installation in working order is at Ismaning.

Activities

These are given in the attached report but are summarised below:-

(1) Research on wave propagation in the case of indirect ray working particularly in connection with Komet navigation system

(2) Research on radar, during recent months only. A contribution to the work by v. Handel and v. Soden on elimination of interference with radar by a frequency modulation process.

(3) The radar system "Sandsknecht" of v. Soden.

(4) Modulation of centimeter waves by ionised gas contained in a glass tube fitting into a cylindrical cavity resonator.

(5) Research on discharge of aircraft static.

(6) Research on great-circle deviations of ionosphere waves and dependence on solar and magnetic conditions.

(7) Analysis, with Kochel station and FFO, by v. Soden and a paper by Dessauer on methods for synchronisation of ground stations (the method used by the Allies not being known).

(8) D/F on kilometer waves, e.g. Rugby on 16 km. Propagation study on a site at Lake Constance. This site used a U-Adcock of 60 meters base with 30 meter masts, the work being done by a Dipl. Ing. Poldena under the direction of Dr. Crone. Started work Dec. 1944.

(9) Preliminary work has been done on the use of the Komet system receiver for accurate direction-finding.

Equipment

The laboratories were well equipped with test gear of all kinds, including much of Italian and French manufacture, and the model-shop contained some 16 lathes and other machine-tools of up-to-date design.

The following are worthy of mention:

(1) Quartz-controlled standard-frequency equipment; fundamental 100 kc/s with decade division down to 1 cycle/sec. and with synchronous clock connected to it.

(2) Slotted concentric measuring lines one meter long, highly engineered, and extremely attractive.

(3) Electronic frequency meter 0 to 60 kc/s by A.E.G. with 6 inch scale.

(4) Dark-room, well fitted. Oscilloscope camera lenses hidden for safety. Some photographic equipment removed by French.

(5) Valves "lighthouse" concentric all ceramic interval anode triodes type LD9 used in 20 cm oscillation for Q measurements.

   NB – This station possesses a book on the whole range of special valves by Telefunken.

Target Information

Dispersals mentioned above have not been examined. The very-long-wave Adcock at Lake Constance and the 6-mast Adcock at Sandsberg have not been examined. Enquiries are Lorenz and Telefunken revealed that Dipl. Ing. Rahn (Telefunken) is held by French, possibly at Diessen on the Ammer See.

Requests by Staff

Dr. Crone urgently requested permission to continue the work on F.M. of pulse which is nearing completion, on behalf of the Allies.

REPORT IX

Investigation of Versuchstation Herzogstand, Kochel
(ionospheric research station)

Date   26th May 1945

Investigators:

S/L. Farvis	T.R.E.
Lt. Redgment	A.S.E.
Capt. Snowden	R.R.DE.
Mr. Hansel	R.C.A.

Personnel Interrogated: Dipl. Phys. John Petersen.

The station is run by Dipl. Phys. John Petersen, with Dr. Eyfrig and 3 other men assistants plus 2 women assistants and is an out-station of the Ferdinand Braun Institut.

A brief history of the station is that it was taken over from Lorenz by Prof. Zenneck of Technische Hochschule Munich, in 1930. Prof. Zenneck ran it as an ionospheric research out-station of the Technische Hochschule, with Dr. Goubau as his assistant. Dr. Goubau is now Professor at Jena where he succeeded Professor Esau. Petersen came in 1935. In 1939 the station was taken over by the Deutsche Versuchsanstalt fur Luftfahrt to screen the personnel from military service since the information provided was of use to the state (Prof. v. Handel was a member of the DVL). When in 1943 Prof. Von Handel was given the Ferdinand Braun Institute the station became part of the Institute.

Until 1937 soundings were taken at fixed frequencies only, working with Berlin DVF for oblique measurements, then in 1937 Dr. Goubau built the continuously variable automatic equipment for 1 - 10 Mc/s which is now in use. The P.R.F. is 50 c/s, power output 200 watts into 2 horizontal dipoles, 1-3 Mc/s (slung between hillsides) and 3-10 Mc/s. (The dipoles are made of the cage type and a new one is just being erected with a 2 metre cage). Pulse length approx. 100 microseconds.

The present scheme is to take measurements every 15 minutes (automatically throughout the 24 hours) and record on film. There are complete film records for the last 14 years.

Since 1939 results in standard tabular form have been passed to Zentralstelle fur Funkberatung near Ried. (a freq. advice bureau founded by the Luftwaffe and later taken over by the Army). Other ionospheric stations reporting to this Zentralstelle were:

Leobersdorf
Oslo
Merkiselfrieden
Tromso
Nikolait
Caucasus Mts
Athens
Syracuse
Medon (France)
Angers (France)
Kulingsborn
Liegefeld (near Weimar)
Koln
Rome

Equipment:

The 200 watt transmitter completes the automatic sweep from 1 to 10 Mc/s in 4 minutes. Common T and R working is employed and the block schematic diagram is given:

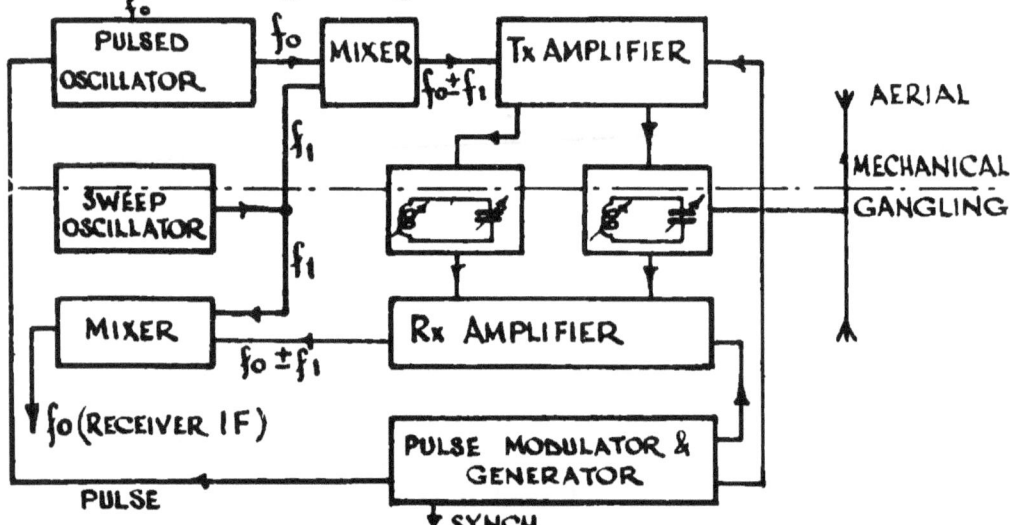

The tunes R/F circuits are common to the T and R the amplifier which is not required being suppressed. During the transmission of the pulse the receiver is paralysed and the transmitter amplifier freed; before the pulse returns from the ionosphere the transmitter has been cut-off and the receiver becomes operative.

The major part of the receiver selectivity is in the IF amplifier. The ganging is performed mechanically by means of cams. To obtain the wide tuning range both L and C are varied, 0 - 180° of the condenser being used for one range, and 180° - 360° being used for the second range, where a different set of inductances have been brought into circuit. Variable inductance is obtained by using the rotors of variometers, whose stators are rocked by cams to give the required time variation of frequency.

The recording mechanism consists of a camera which is slowly traversed across a cathode ray tube; a number of records are placed on one film.

A new transmitter, giving 800 watts and covering up to 20 Mc/s is under construction. For experimental work a transportable equipment was being built in a rack approx. 4 ft. x 2 ft. x 1 ft.

Results

All the results except the film records were removed by Major Kojan, U.S. Signal Corps, and taken to the Interservices Ionospheric Bureau at Gt. Baddow, Essex.

Publications:

All the recent publications were removed by Major Kojan, with the results. Some which were not taken are listed below:

1. Mitteilung der deutschen Akademie der Luftfahrtforschung
    Band 2   1943 Hefr 2
2. Deutche Luftforschung. Forsching Bericht u. 1943
3. Probleme u. Ergebnisse der Ionosphere from Jenaische
    Zeitschrift fur Medezin u. Naturwissenschaft Band 77
    1944.
4. HFT   1940   Vol 56   pp   129-136
5. HFT   1943   Vol 62   Heft 5.   M 137
6. HFT   1936   Vol 48   M 7-21
7. HFT   1940   Vol 55   M 86-94
8. Die Naturwissenschaften 1942   30 Jahrgang Heft 50/51
9. Schriften der Deutschen Akademie der Luftfahrtforschung
    1943 Band 7 Heft 1. Uber die Tagliche
    Schwankungen in Zustand der F-Schicht
10. Schriften der Deutschen Akademie der Luftfahrtforschung
    1944 Band 8 Heft 1.
11. Schriften der Deutschen Akademie der Luftfahrtforschung
    1944 Band 8 Heft 1.
12. Schriften der Deutschen Akademie der Luftfahrtforschung
    1942 Heft 51 Pg 1
13. Schriften der Deutschen Akademie der Luftfahrtforschung
    1940 31st May Pg 43
14. Ferdinand Braun Inst. (not published) "Inwieweit lasst
    die Tagesziffen B (number supplied by Prof. Bartels from
    his Magnetical observatory at Potsdam) auf der
    Abendkongentration Schliessen"
15. Beitrage zur Erfassung der Breiten Abhangigheit der EM
    Konzentration der F_2 Shicht 18 July 1942 not published
16. Eine neue darstellumgform von Ionsphorergebnissen
    Oct 1944 by Eyfrig
17. Vergleich der Ionspharergebnissen der Versuchsstation
    Herzogstand mit deren des N.B.S. Washington Feb 1942.

18. (Zentralstelle) Forschungsbericht Nr 1941
19.   "   "   Nr 782
20.   "   "   Nr 1809
21.   "   "   Nr 826
22. Die Wissenschaftlichen Unterlage fur die
    Konstruktion eines Frequenzschiebere bezuglich
    der F schicht (Eyfrig) not published 25 Oct 1943.

Astronomical data was obtained as required from Herr Brunner in Switzerland, and from the Fraunhofer Inst. in Frieburg. There is a recording astronomical station on the top of the Wendelstein near Brannenburg.

Recommendation

It is strongly recommended that this station be allowed to continue its routine ionospheric sounding work in order to provide its results to the Allies.

                      Lt. Redgment
                      S/L. Farvis

Project 1.

B. ERNST ORLICH INSTITUTE

REPORT I.

Mechanical Vibrators as Filters for Harmonics.

A) Project was suggested in 1940 or 1941 bei Heereswaffenamt WaPrüf 7-IV.

B) Theoretical and experimental work.

C) Dr. Faulstich. -

D) Tuningfork standard frequency transmitter with temperature control. Special cathode ray oscillograph. Audio-frequency transmitter for precision-tuning. Screened boxes for holding the vibrating elements with exciting and pick-up headings. Steel strips and nickel rods with tubes as vibrating elements. Wien-Robinson Bridge for frequency-metering. Auxiliary transmitters, amplifiers, phones and the like.

All of this equipment has as yet not been evacuated from Wolfersdorf, except an auxilliary transmitter with power pack and some magnetizing coils for nickel rods.

E) The project aims at establishing filtering equipment, by which the harmonics of a fundamental frequency chosen at will within a certain small range can sharply be picked up out of any mixture of frequencies. Mechanical systems, able to oscillate in various modes with different frequencies are used as oscillating circuits. They are tuned to the fundamental frequency by superimposed stresses, corrected to the ideal law of harmonics by mechanical loading or cutting, excited by suitably arranged exciting coils and provided with thoroughly discoupled pick-ups. Influence of quality, phase shift, and undesired coupling between different modes of oscillating are investigated.

F) Theoretical and experimental investigations on transverse vibrating steel strips incl. corrective loading to realise ideal harmonic law are completed.
Theoretical considerations on longitudinal magnetostrictive excitation of nickel tubes and rods almost completed. Experimental work with regard to deviations from ideal law advanced. Methods of cutting to arrive at ideal law under consideration. Measurements of phase shift and quality for the magnetostrictive device and fundamental considerations on other kinds of mechanical vibrators (diaphragms, air-columns, cavities and so on) outstanding and desirable.

G) Completed part of work concerning the steel strip vibrator was published about 1 or 2 years ago as part of a paper of Dr. Faulstiche.

"Electromechanical Filter Equipment for Damping Hum arising from Harmonics of a 50 c/s Supply".

The paper is evacuated from Wolfersdorf in 9 copies and listed under C.1 and O.5.

Project 2.

ERNST ORLICH INSTITUTE

Extirpation of Hum by Mechanical Resonant Filters.

A) Project was suggested in 1940 or 1941 bei Heereswaffenamt WaPruf 7 - IV.

B) Theoretical and experimental work.

C) Dr. Faulstich.

D) Steel-strip with screening box, tuning handle, exciting and pick-up coils; special amplifier to correct for different phase shift and amplitude for the harmonics dealt with, suited to normal knapsack-equipment of the German army.

All of this equipment has been handed to the Heereswaffenamt, which wanted to carry out informative tests with the equipment; it has therefore not been evacuated from Wolfersdorf.

E) Transverse oscillating steel strips (see Project I) are tuned to a fundamental frequency of 50 c/s or the frequency of the supply concerned by means of precision setting of its internal stress. The tensions picked up from the oscillating strip are amplified in a 3 stage amplifier, with corrective elements for stage coupling to account for the differences in amplitude and phase of the strip-tension output due to the differences in quality. The output of the amplifier is connected in counter series to the input voltage, thus removing the harmonics to a high degree (10% remaining) without impairing language. To be used for normal knapsack equipment for listening by means of earthed soundings instead of hitherto employed electrical filters.

F) Entirely completed. Device has been delivered. Tests have given satisfactory results.
Should practical use be taken into consideration, development of the device to meet practical requirements with regard to sturdy and narrow design would be advisable. Further decrease of level of harmonics and extension up to higher orders seems to be within the scope of the project, would however require further theoretical and experimental investigation.

G) Completed about 1 or 2 years ago. Published as second part of a paper presented by Dr. Faulstich.

"Electromechanical Filter Equipment for Damping Hum arising from Harmonics of 50 c/s Supply"

The paper has been evacuated from Wolfersdorf in 9 copies and has been listed under C1 and O5.

Project 3.

Mechanical Resonant Filters as Anti-jamming for RADAR.
Codename (Kamm)

A) Official order was given by the "Bevollmachtigter der Hochfrequenzforschung (BHF) "acting on behalf of the "Forschungsführung des Reichsministers der Luftfahrt und Oberbefehlshabers der Luftwaffe". The order was given in 1944, though the work was begun in the preceding year.

B) Theoretical and experimental work.

C) Dr. Faulstich and Dipl. Ing. Reichardt.

D) In order to select the useful reflected signals out of jamming signals, which normally are not coherent with the right ones, a mechanical resonant system (magnetostrictive nickel rod) is used according to the fundamental considerations set forth in project 1. Even as well a odd harmonics up to the 60th order of the rod must be used in order to arrive at the accuracy of distance metering desired, the pulse frequency being controlled by the fundamental of the rod. Tuning is affected by homogeneous premagnetizing, adjusting of the harmonic law by cutting and/or homogeneous demagnetizing. Difference in the resonant properties due to quality are smoothed by the coupling elements of a multi-stage amplifier.

F) Theoretical work almost completed.
Experimental work with regard to law of harmonics, quality and phase shift advanced. 40th to 50th harmonic reached.
Amplifier for output under construction.
Further experimental work for matching parts together and to the RADAR equipment necessary; extension to 60th harmonic desirable. Simple and reliable method of cutting the rod or tube to proper harmonic law wanted, which requires further experimental work, that has just been begun.

G) Not completed. No reports available except short provisional notes fixed up weekly by the investigators. These notes have not been found during the inspection in Wolfersdorf, they might perhaps have been inserted in personal files of the investigators.

D) Audio frequency transmitters of different types. Premagnetizing coils. These parts have been transferred to T-Branch G-2 Wiesbaden and are classified under C1 to 6 in the list of evacuated material. Nickel rods and tubes of proper dimensions with holding equipment, exciting coils, pick-ups, demagnetizing coils, special amplifier, cathode ray oscillograph, output meter, and normal accessories have not been evacuated as yet.

Project 4.

Pulse Modulating as a Means of Removing RADAR - Disturbances due to Window.
Codename - Rotlaus.

A) The project was suggested by the "Bevollmachtigter der Hochfrequenzforschung" in 1944.

B) Theortical and practical work.

) German design of Rotterdam-Equipment i.e. H_2S. The device with all necessary accessories was moved from Danzig to the Reichsstelle in Berlin- Gatow in the beginning of February. From thence it was erroneously shipped to Ulm-Dornstadt in March. So far I am informed it has reached neither Dornstadt, nor Wolfersdorf. Pulse generator, special cathode ray oscillograph for pulses, additional automatic frequency adjusting device for auxiliary oscillator of the Rotterdam. All of these devices were almost completed. The final work was to be done by the personnel left in Travesmunde, where the equipment should still be available. Pulse analyser. This device, too, was under construction in Travemunde and should be found there. For further details see Project 38(G) Tube for load modulation of main signal connected to branch of antenna feeder. First design was evacuated from Wolfersdorf to T-Branch G-2 in Wisbaden.

C) Dipl.Ing.Hollmann and Dr. Faulstich (cand.electr. Dreyer and Vesper)

E) Radially moving reflectors such as planes can be separated from fixed reflectors such as window by superimposing the reflected signals on the signal of an auxiliary transmitter coherent in phase. At Hyperfrequency this method fails on account of the difficulties involved in establishing the phase coherence. In our project the main pulses of 3000 mc/s were to be modulated by means of a diode controlled by a 25 Mc/s transmitter. The auxiliary oscillator of the main equipment should be shifted to 3015 Mc/s, thus originating two intermediate frequencies of 10 and 15 mc/s with the upper sideband and the carrier of the signals. With a band width of the normal receiver of 6 Mc/s no changes to this amplifier are needed except exact adjustment of the 15 Mc/s difference to the carrier.

F) Theoratical considerations of the problem had essentially been completed.
The Rotterdam equipment of normal design was studied and had been worked over to meet practical service conditions.
The main parts for the experimental work were approaching completion.
The essential work still to be executed comprises; Testing of the different auxiliary parts and assembly of the equipment as a whole for final tests.

(G) In January 1945 a provisional report on the theoretical considerations and the conclusions arrived at has been prepared by one of the investigators (Dipl.Ing.Hollmann). A small number of copies of this paper has been sent to interested people including the BHF and the Research Dept., of the German Ministry of Aircraft. No copy was found Wolfersdorf.

Project 5.

Guiding beam System at 600 mc/s for Remote-controlled Rockets.
Codenames:- Libelle and Gloria.

A) The project was suggested by the "Bevollmachtigter der Hochfrequenzforschung (BHF) on behalf of the Research laboratories of the V.2 Department of the Heereswaffenamt in Peenemunde. The order was given in 1944.

B) Theoretical and practical work.

C) Dipl.Ing.Battac, Dr. Faulstich and cand.electr.Goedecke.

E) V.2. Rockets have hitherto been controlled with ultra short waves. Such a type of device can easily be jammed. In order to ensure a higher degree of reliability of the control a decrease in wavelength was considered. It was intended to make use of the normal equipment in the rocket adding a simple hyperfrequency receiver with a primary bandfilter circuit tuned to 2 frequencies the difference of which equals the prior receiver frequency. The normal receiver now acts as an intermediate frequency stage of the whole equipment. The "Gloria" order related to the testing of the hyperfrequency link, which was designed by a factory. In order to evade the difficulties of stablizing the auxiliary frequency inside the rocket, it was intended to have an auxiliary frequency to form the intermediate frequency in the receiver transmitted from a ground transmitter. The order "Libelle" included advisory work with regard to the ground equipment (Antennas, transmitter) as well as the design of the phase shifting for the beam antennae equipment. A detour line in the concentric cable feeder for the antennae inserted and short-circuited consecutively was thought most advantageous and was under construction.

D) Measuring line for the dm-range delivered from Konstanz was tested in Travemünde and should still be there.
Precision measuring line should have been completed in the mean time for the dm-range which was under construction in Travemunde.
Noise generator was prepared in Travemunde.
All accessories too had still been left in Travemunde. Order for moving to Wolfersdorf had been given, but did probably not reach Travemunde on account of difficulties in transport.
Nothing of the equipment involved was found in Wolfersdorf.

F) Gloria. Preliminary tests for one set of the receiver have been carried out with fairly satisfying results. Further sets for thorough investigations were to be delivered by the factory, but did not arrive until the date of April 15th.
Libelle. Design for the revolving switch for the detour line was completed, the switch with all accessories was under construction in Travemünde

Theory. Theoretical considerations were advances.

G) Work was not completed. The theoretical considerations involved have been presented to the Heereswaffenamt and to the BHF by the head of the institute, Prof. Dr. Schwenkhagen. The copy of this paper, apparently has been destroyed in Wolfersdorf.

Project 6

Measuring in the 500 to 5000 Mc/s band.

A) No special order was given to the laboratory. The work relating to this object was done without written agreement relying on personal discussions with the Branches of the BHF concerned.

B) Mainly experimental work.

C) Dr. Faulstich, Dipl. Ing. Bettac, Dipl. Ing. Schmunde. Dr. Mohr, Dipl. Ing. Eider.

D) 2 measuring lines of the concentric cable type had been designed and were completed. They are or should be in Travemunde. 2 measuring lines of the wave-guide type for the cm-range were under construction. Part of them was in Travemunde, other parts in Wolfersdorf. They have as yet not been evacuated. Additional equipment such as a hyperfrequency signal transmitter, harmonic generators, detector-voltmeters, matching lines (detours and branches) were designed and almost completed. None of these parts were seen in Wolfersdorf except some spare tubes.

E) At the time being our work was still confined to testing our own equipment with regard to accuracy, proper function, calibrating and so on. These tests completed, further work had to be done along the line of determining the properties of supports, bushings, joints, plugs, bents, branches, transforming elements and other similar parts especially for the range of 10 to 30 cm wave-length which was not covered in Germany. A further object of our investigations was to be the development of a "through-put-meter" ie. a non-absorbing power-metering device for hyperfrequency. A separate order of the BHF for this part of the research was pending.

F) As mentioned above under D most of the necessary equipment for the main work was prepared and approaching completion. Continuation of the work in the intermediate range, where wave-guides as well as concentric cables can be used and must often be coupled together, seems to be desirable.
So far as we can see, there is a definite need for the "through-put-meter" for the whole waveband concerned. So this device should be cultivated preferably.

G) No reports with regard to the experimental work have as yet been given only short weekly summaries of my associates, which still may be found in their personal files. Not removed from Wolfersdorf. The head of the institute, Prof. Dr. Schwenkhagen has presented some papers for the instruction of the associates as "Hausberichte".

1) Lines used as transformers and measuring elements.
2) Fundamental laws of wave propagation in a delectric layer.
3) Fundamental laws of wave-propagation in a circular tube.
4) Fundamental laws of wave-propagation in rectangular tubes.
5) Properties of resonating circuits for Hyperfrequency.

Paper nr.1. was evacuated from Wolfersdorf and listed in Wiesbaden at the T-branch office under Nr.V.1.
2 and 3 have been in Wolfersdorf but were not found, spare copies should be in Travemunde, together with the manuscript for 4. The manuscript for 5 is in Parsan near Vorsfelde, not far from Braunschweig.

Project 7.

Electric and Magnetic Property measurements up to very high frequencies

A) This project was suggested by the "Bevollmachtigter der Hochfrequenzforschung (BHF) in 1944, written order was pending.

B) Experimental work

C) Dipl. Ing. Karl Roewer, cand. el. Schroeder
In chemical questions Prof. Dr. Klemm, Head of the Chemical Laboratory of the Technische Hochschule Danzig, was collaborating with us.

D) Measuring section for concentric cable line under constructions in Travemunde. Signal transmitters, wavelength metering equipment, audio frequency bridge devices. Pressing arrangements for the dusty material. Partly to be found in Travemunde, the rest in Wolfersdorf. Nothing has been taken to Wiesbaden. Materials to be tested might be found at the laboratory of Prof. Klemm in Schmalkalden (Thuringen)

E) Protective coatings to diminish the reflective power of planes and submarines were taken into consideration (Codenames: Schwarzes Flugzeug and Schornsteinfeger). Materials for this purpose should have elevated permeability and dielectric constant, the quotient of these properties remaining equal to that of air. These materials should have moderate dielectric and magnetic losses to an amount as equal as possible. The institute was to give the necessary experimental help for measuring these properties to the chemists preparing the stuff, esp. to Prof. Klemm mentioned above and to the laboratories of the I.G.Farben in Hochst working for this project.

F) Preliminary tests have been carried out for lower frequencies up to some 100 Kc/s with probes handed to us by Prof. Klemm to find out to what extent and along what laws the properties of the probes would depend upon the pressure they had been exposed to when pressed into the proper shape for metering. The relations between frequency and apparent values of properties had been studied too. With hyperfrequency equipment completed now, the investigation on appropriate lines can be carried on.

G) Not completed. No report available as yet.

Project 8.

Causes of atmospherics - How to Quench them

A) This project was first suggested by the Deutsche Versuchsanstalt fur Luftfahrt (DVL) in 1940 acting on behalf of E.4-Department of the Reichsluftfahrtministerium. Later on additional orders for this project were given by the Forschungsfurung des Reichsministers der Luftfahrt und Oberbefehlshabers der Luftwaffe and by the Heereswaffenamt WaPruf 7.

B) Practical research work, recording of natural phenomena and laboratory tests. Additional theoretical considerations.

C) Dr.Weinhold Dipl.Ing.Tschikste, Dipl.Ing.Dreike, Dipl.Ing.Pohl. cand.electr.Ursih. and electr. Wolfartsberger.

D) Generating voltmeters with amplifiers evacuated from Wolfersdorf and listed in T-Branch G-2 in Wiesbaden under G I to 8. Receiver with special output amplifier for recording was not found in Wolfersdorf, might be picked up in Travemunde. Various antennas of normal and special design (were left in Danzig). Recording equipment for antenna d.c. with Hisentroll. Not evacuated from Wolfersdorf, perhaps to be found in Travemunde.
Calibrating transmitter for recording equipment, evacuated and listed in Wiesbaden under D.3 and 4. Pulse generator evacuated, listed D.1. Various normal receivers such as FuG X, Fug XVI, FuG XVII, and knapsack receivers of the army. As yet not evacuated. Locating equipment for atmospherics (Adcock) with special indicator tube and photographic recording. Parts left in Danzig, parts of the rest evacuated from Wolfersdorf (List D.2.) recording camera still in Wolf.

E) According to the result of the investigations, three main types of atmospherics must be considered. 1) Hissing, which is not due to precipitation as most of the experts are believing, but is a mere static problem due to excessive potential gradient in the atomosphere causing periodical breakdown. It can be removed by electrostatic shielding of the antenna. 2) Pulses are due to atmospherics discharge, i.e., to lightning flashes, which however, contrary to normal opinion, need not always be visible, or be accompanied by thunder. Their disturbing influence to wireless communications can be lowered considerably by quenching equipment in receiving sets. 3) Grinders are very similar to thermal noises. In the low frequency range they are mainly due to a rapid sequence of clic-pulses, in the high frequency range extra-terrestrial causes must be taken into account. They are the very limit for useful amplification of a receiver.

F) Hissing and the countermeasures against this type of statics are essentially cleared up. The cause of clics and a number of methods to remove them in reception are known. With regard to this work a final experimental investigation comparing the efficacity and the draw backs of all methods seems to be highly desirable. For the grinders nothing except some orienting tests has been done as yet. Their investigation for the whole frequency range of telecommunications ought to be of the utmost importance.

G) Part of the results of our investigations has been laid down in papers published by the ZWB. Their titles are:-

1) Hissing
2) Recording of Atmospherics at 6 Mc/S
3) Device for Recording the level of clicks and Results for 1942 to 1944.
4) Report on the Meeting: Level of Atmospherics.

The reports numbers 1 to 3 above were presented by Dr.Meinhold the report nr.4. gives the survey of all practical work done in this field in Germany gathered in a meeting held under the direction of Prof. Dr. Sohwenkhagen who signed the report. All these reports were evacuated from Wolfersdorf and brought to T-Branch G-2 Wiesbaden, where they have been listed under D7, D8, and D 10 a and b respectively.

Further papers are under preparation:

5) The design of anti-hissing Antennas
6) Contributions to the laws of hissing
7) Proposals for standard Nomenclature of Interference.

Files, notes, lists of experimental results have been evacuated from Wolfersdorf and are in the hands of Prof. Dr. Sohwenkhagen. It is desirable to have them completed.

Project 9.

Additional information on Atmospheric Electricity
Codename Windmuhle

A) In 1942 the Forschungsfuhrung des Reichsministers der Luftfahrt und Oberbefehlshabers der Luftwaffe gave the formal order for this project, which had already been considered prior to this date. In the meantime the project has often been dropped for months to push on with other work.

B) Experimental research of natural data.

C) Dr. Meinhold, Dipl.Ing.Dreike, Miss Seiz, Prof.Dr.Mehmel.

D) Generating voltmeters and additional equipment were removed from Wolfersdorf and listed in Wiesbaden in the T Branch G-2 Office under G 1 to 7. Special installations in the W 34 or Do.17 plane of the institute. (might be found in Altenburg or in Travemunde). Special condenser design for measuring polar conductivity of the atmosphere, highly sensitive galvometers and hisentrolls for high input resistance (Not evacuated from Wolfersdorf).

E) Records of the potential gradient of the atmospheric field have been taken in Danzig for more than one year almost continuously. They should be prepared with regard to fieldstrength, fluctuations, of field strength and sign with the meteorological dates gathered for the same period. This should give the base for evaluating the real cause of a considerable part of this field. In addition hereto an investigation of the charge spaces occurring in the atmosphere near the ground as well as in the free space especially in clouds was prepared. First results have been gathered. In addition the Measurement of polar electric conductivity of air and an analysis of the kind of ions involved was considered.

F) Records are taken; comparing them with weather conditions has been started with preliminary results. Tests for measuring the space charge by means of generating Voltmeters inside a Faraday cage have successfully been started. The measurement of conductivity is under design. Continuation of the work would be very interesting from a fundamental standpoint, especially with regard to the question of the origin of thunder-storm electricity.

G) Not completed. Part of the results gathered as yet have been used for the investigation of project 12. The rest is not published and should not be published before additional evaluation has been possible. Further records might turn out to be required. The majority of the results as yet obtained have been removed from Wolfersdorf and are in the hands of Prof. Dr. Schwenkhagen.

Project 10.

How to use Atmospherics for Weather Forecasts

A) The investigation of this project was done according to appointments made with Prof. Dr. Plötze, Associate of the Department Skl 6 of the Oberkommando der Kriegsmarine with the agreement of the Bevollmachtigter der Hochfrequenzforschung (BHF). It was started in 1944.

B) Gathering of experimental data and evaluation of the results.

C) Dr. Meinhold, Prof. Mehmel, Dipl.Ing.Tschikste, Miss Seiz.

D) Direction finding equipment for atmospherics for 3 wavelengths with ink pen recorder has been left in Wolfersdorf.
Direction finding equipment of Italian design (Prof.Ranzi) was being installed near Travemunde under the direction of Mr. Tschikste and should still be there. Two similar sets were to be delivered to be installed in different places to make up a location finding grid system. Probably, the delivery has not been executed.

E) Our feeling that atmospherics could be used as an auxiliary source of information for forecasting weather is based upon the definite belief in each click originating from a tropospheric discharge. Such discharges (see project 8) are always bound to areas frequently having air masses of high humidity. The evaluation of the directional distribution recorded in Danzig with the direction finder of Lugeon-Nobile mentioned above gave evidence that orographic conditions play an important part in the activity of the "front". From Danzig fronts could be perceived during their movement from the Atlantic coast on to the Urals Speed of propagation of electric activity seem to be correlated.

F) The first results are promising. The experimental work should aim at finding our best frequencies for the purpose of forecasting and should include the erection of at least 3 identical stations of properly designed recording apparatus, with sufficient length of base. The direction finding equipment of the Reichsamt fur Wetterdienst designed for the location of single pulses might be taken into consideration, too.

G) Not finally completed. The results gathered as yet have been compiled for the manuscript of a paper of Prof. Dr. Mehmel.

> Contributions to the relations between the direction and a distribution of Atmospherics in Danzig and the meteorological conditions on the continent.

The paper is about half completed. The main part of the manuscript and notes for it have been removed from Wolfersdorf and are in the hands of Prof. Dr. Schwenhagen.

Project 11

Dry Textile Discharger for Planes

A) Work on this project was done in connection with the Department GL-CE 5 of the "Reichsminister der Luftfahrt und Oberbefehls- haber der Luftwaffe" and in collaboration with the Deutsche Lufthansa"

B) Practical work exclusively.

C) Dr. Meinhold and cand. el. Wolfartsberger

D) Hemp thread coated with Dissultol-varnish. Rectifier for High tension d.c. with power pack. Commercial receiving set with output meter. This equipment has as yet now been removed from Wolfersdorf.

E) A hemp thread of about 5" length coated with carbon by varnishing it with Dissultol, a suspension of graphite in some volatile liquid, has proved to be a very efficient discharger for static charging. Currents up to about 100 MA are removed without causing appreciable interference. Comparative tests have shown its superiority to the tungsten point suggested by the DVL and in practical use at the Deutsche Lufthansa with regard to interference for most discharge currents concerned. It is less expensive than all other kind of dischargers and needs less maintenance. Flight tests have not been carried on far enough to decide the period of useful life of the device.

F) The discharger has been tested in the laboratory. After flight tests carried out by the Deutsche Lufthansa for 25 hours the discharger become ineffective owing to the coating being wiped off by the airstream and corresponding increase in resistance. Further testing with regard to useful time of life and the wearing process under flight conditions are necessary. Tests with artificial textile fibres with inherent internal conductivity instead of the surface conductivity used now are desirable.

G) First design completed. Results have been summarized in a report given by Dr. Meinhold.

> New type of Discharger for removing Static Charges from planes.

This paper has been evacuated from Wolfersdorf and is listed as D.18 in the list of papers of T Branch G 2 in Wiesbaden.

Project 12.

Can Atmospheric Electricity Upset the Control of Projectiles Telecontrolled by Wires

Codename – Fritz X and X.4

A) This project was suggested by the Electrical Department of the "Deutsche Versuchsanstalt fur Luftfahrt (DVL)" in 1942

B) Theoretical considerations and experimental work.

C) Dipl.Ing.Pohl, Dipl, Ing. Dreike, Dr. Meinhold.

D) Sounding balloons, Kite-Balloons, special wiring, spilling equipment, The equipment referred to in connection with the projects 8 and 9 has been used for this project too. The equipment has not been evacuated from Wolfersdorf.

E) With test bombings carried out with telecontrolled bombs like Fritz X troubles had been experiences which were attributed by experts to the influence of the atmospheric electric field. This project was to clear up the possibilities of such influence. Information found in prior literature and own measurements carried out to complete this information hitherto available gave the necessary fundamentals for evaluating the influence of potential gradient, space charge, field breaks and currents due to the conductivity of the air. It is concluded that with an appropriate design no real trouble need be feared.

F) Investigation completed in 1945 Further information with regard to density of space charge desirable (see project 9)

G) Completed in the beginning of 1945. The conclusions have been compiled to a paper presented by Prof. Sohwenkhagen and Dr. Meinhold.

Can Atmospheric Electricity Upset the Control of Projectiles Telecommanded by Wires?

This paper completed in German Language and ready for being copied, has been translated into English too and might be typed from the manuscripts. The German and the English texts have been evacuated from Wolfersdorf and are in the hands of Prof. Schwenkhagen.

Project 13

Limitations of Electrostatic Proximity Fuses due to Atmospheric Electricity

Codename: Kuhglocke

A) This project was suggested by the Sonderkommision fur Zunderfragen beim Reichsminister fur Rustung und Kriegproduktion (SKfz)". The formal order was pending. Suggestion was made early in 1945.

B) Theoretical considerations based upon the experimental data available in connection with project 12.

C) Dipl. Ing. Pohl. Dr. Meinhold. Prof. Schwenkhagen.

D) Nothing but the equipment mentioned in connection with project 12

E) Electrostatic proximity fuses are operated by the electric field surrounding a plane due to the charges normally found on its surface on account of the combustion process or to taking over space charges. They are liable to faulty operation caused by the elements of atmospheric electricity, such as; potential gradient and its sudden changes due to discharges, space charge, conductivity of the air causing current. The project is to discuss all of these possibilities and to compare the level of the useful signals due to a plane with the level disturbances due to meteorological elements.

F) The basic information used for project 12 give sufficient data for fixing the considerations, which as yet, have not been laid down in writing. They have only been discussed among the investigators. Exact calculations of the various influences and writing of the manuscript have still to be done.

G) No paper available, because work is incomplete.

Project 14

Contributions to the Knowledge of so-called Precipitation-Statics

A) This work was suggested by the "Forschungsfuhrung des Reichsministers der Luftfahrt und Oberbefanhlhabers der Luftwaffe" in 1943 or 44

B) Mainly experimental work involved.

C) Dr. Meinhold, cand.el.Wolfartsberger. Valuable assistance has been given to us by Dipl.Ing.Matschull, associate of Prof.Dr. Seiz, head of the high tension Laboratory of the Technische Hochschule Danzig.

D) High tension rectifier with power pack such as is mentioned in connection with project II, Moving coil oscillograph, cathode ray oscillograph. Frequency metering equipment, receiver and outputmeter. None of this equipment has been removed from Wolfersdorf.

E) Though the physical cause of Hissing or Precipitation Static has been fully discovered by our work (see project 8), not sufficient information is available with regard to the full mechanism of the discontinuous discharge to the atmosphere from the point of the aerial. This project is to cover this gap from a general viewpoint taking into account the dimensions of the antenna as well as the conditions and properties of the air surrounding the aerial and the stage of the surface. If possible it was intended to explain the frequency of hissing and the different behaviour of hissing for different sign of potential gradients from the general laws of gaseous discharges.

F) Quite a lot of experimental research has been done in the winter 1944 to 1945 in the laboratory. Additional tests in the open air under normal weather conditions, were under preparation for the summer 1945, but could not be accomplished. Further research would be highly desirable from a scientific standpoint.

G) The experimental data gathered giving valuable information from a phenomenological point of view even without full theoretical understanding of the causes involved, it has been decided to enter them into a survey, which is partly completed. The necessary information in their main parts have been evacuated from Wolfersdorf and are in the hands of Prof. Schwenkhagen.

Project 15

Fundamental Investigations on Magnetically Homing Torpedoes

Codename: Marchen

A) This project was suggested by the "Torpedo-Versuchsanstalt der Deutschen Kriegsmarine" in 1944.

B) Theoretical work as well as experimental research and practical testing involved.

C) Dipl.Ing.Hollman, cand. el. Kerkovius, Dipl.Ing.Stange.

D) Hisentrolls and Hisenverts (see project 39 and 40) special moving coil oscillograph for recording purposes (torpedo-oscillograph), torpedo with electrical drive, spare parts of torpedoes Hosentrolls and Hisenverts have been evacuated. The torpedo oscillograph has been left in Wolfersdorf. The torpedoes had been returned to the TVA in Gotenhafen in February 1945.

E) The Hisentroll offering a new type of highly sensitive, but mechanically reliable d.c. operated controlling device. (see project 39) opened the chance of magnetically homing torpedoes. The theoretical considerations showed that with a sensitivity of 10^{-15} Watt input offered by Hisentrol a weight of 50 to 100 lb. installed as two astatic windings on the heading and the tail of the torpedo would be sufficient to give rise to the first controlling pulse at distances of 250 to 300 yards. The experimental work was to find an answer to the question of the level of disturbing signals arising from the movements of the torpedo in the goemagnetic field and from changes in condition of its own magnetic properties. The experiments have shown that these influences are limiting the distance range to something like 20 to 30 yards, just sufficient for a proximity fuse which, however, was not considered.

F) Full theoretical survey of the distance range given by sensitivity, weight of material and dimensions of the torpedo available. Valuable information with regard to the behaviour of iron structures when moving in the magnetic field. Sufficient for the decision to be taken with regard to magnetically homing torpedoes: nevertheless, further experiments are desirable on account of the importance of the questions involved for the magnetic compasses used for commercial ships and aircraft.

G) The work was dropped in October or November 1944, because we had found that no homing would be achieved with the present type of torpedoes. The informations for the final report have been left in the hand of Dipl.Ing.Hollmann and of Dipl.Ing.Stange, who were in charge of it.

Project 16.

Magnetic Proximity Release for Tank-Destroying Rockets Fired by Planes

Codename: Isegrim

A) This project was suggested by the GL CE-9 Department of the Reichsminister der Lufthart and Oberbefehlshaber der Luftwaffe in the end of 1944. The work was done with agreement of the "Bevellmachtigter der Hochfrequenzforschung (BHF)"

B) A little theoretical work, mainly practical experiments.

C) Dipl. Ing. Kober and Dipl. Ing. Stange.

D) Special Hisenvert with power pack has been evacuated from Wolfersdorf. Moving coil oscillograph of Askania-make (Torpedo oscillograph) has been left there. So have been supports for test coils, camera equipment for camera-shooting and similar accessories.

E) Tanks are deforming the geomagnetic field in their neighbourhood. Such deformation can be used to operate the release of rockets from tubes vertically mounted in the wings of a plane when passing overhead of the tank by means of the tension F in 2 coils connected in counter series and translated into the releasing pulse by means of a Hisentrol. (See project 39). The main problem is avoiding faulty pulses due to vibrations; tests have especially been carried out to diminish the microphonic effect of the first tube. Theoretical considerations have found the distance range to be expected to be of the order of 12 to 15 yards.

F) Theoretical considerations are almost complete. Experimental work has resulted in the successful design of a Hisenvert for measuring purposes with a sensitivity superior to that needed for the Hisentroll release equipment with a rate of faulty pulses inferior to 1 in 1000. Camera shooting from a plane as a control of theoretical considerations was under preparation. The influence of magnetized parts of the plane upon the pick-up coils was still to be investigated. The design of such type Hisentroll would be valuable for other purposes in commercial aircraft too.

G) Not completed. The results gathered as yet could be entered in a provisional report, if and when the information, experimental notes and so on left in the hand of the investigators was available. No material was found in connection with the inspection of the laboratory in June 1945.

Project 17.

Fundamental Considerations on Magnetic Anti-Aircraft Proximity Fuses

Codename: Reineke

A) This project was for the first time raised by the Forschungsfuhrung des Reichsministers der Luftfahrt und Oberbefehlshabers der Luftwaffe. It was afterwards taken up again by Dr. Runge on behalf of the Sonderkommision fur Zinderfragen des Reichsministers fuer Rustung und Kriegsproduktion (SKfZ) First originated in 1943, last order pending.

B) Theoretical considerations based on the knowledge gathered in connection with the projects 15 and 16.

C) Dipl.Ing.Stange, Dipl.Ing.Kober, Prof. Schwenkhagen.

D) No other equipment than mentioned in connection with projects 15 - 16.

E) According to the magnetic dipole moment produced by planes and the limitations imposed on the pick-up system for the magnetic fuses by the size, dimensions and permissible weight of equipment was to give full evidence of this fact and should in the second place discuss the advantages of magnetic fuses over other types with regard to the difficulties of developing countermeasures for either jamming or premature fusing.

F) Theoretical considerations are fixed in personal notes of the investigators and have however not been fully elaborated.

G) Not completed, As soon as the information gathered as yet, can be made available, the final report can be presented.

Project 18.

Magnetically Actuated Alarm System for Areas to be Protected (Codename - Gnom)

A) This project was opened in 1943, when the question was raised by an associate of the "Entmagnetisierungsgruppe" (Demagnetizing group) of the "Superiversuchskommando der Kriegsmarine". Later on the Heereswaffenamt (WaPruf 7) as well as the "Wissenschaftlicher Fuhrungsstab der Kriegsmarine" (Scientific Headquarters of the Navy) became interested in it. Engineers of the Technische Nothilfe too have contacted us to know the results obtained.

B) Practical and theoretical work.

C) Hisentroll and Hisenverts such as evacuated from Wolfersdorf and listed at T-Branch G2 in Wiesbaden under A1 to 7.

D) Dipl. Ing. Kober and Dipl. Ing. Stange.

E) Each kind of vehicle is constituting a magnetic dipole owing to fugitive or permanent magnetization. When moving over a wire forming a horizontally arranged sleev or winding on the ground, it will induce a tension in such turn. This tension is picked up by the Hisentroll to operate the alarm device. The sensitivity of the equipment was sufficient to be operated by a single man carrying a gun or a spade when crossing the wire. Practical limits were set by earth currents due to tramway operation and to s.c. supply network. Routine tests have been carried out in the entrance of the port of Gotenhafen recording each vessel entering the harbour for weeks. To remove trouble that might arise from superposition of tensions due to electrolytic action or to thermocouple a combination of Hisenvert and Hisentroll proved fully effective.

F) A lot of experience has been gathered, which would enable the practical design of such an alarm system. The system has offered a new possibility of metering the magnetic properties of floating structures with a very high degree of accuracy even for traces of magnetism left. There is still one question left without an answer by the experiment which would be very interesting from a general point of view. Which tensions are induced in a huge turn of say 1 square mile by slow or sudden changes of the geomagnetic field. In Danzig provision had been made for such tests.

G) Not completed. A paper discussing the limits of an alarm system against tanks has been presented to the Heerswaffenamt. It has not been evacuated from Wolfersdorf. Perhaps the necessary information for rewriting it could be got from the investigators.

Project 19.

Magnetic shielding in the Low Frequency Range

A) This project has been investigated in connection with the design of Hisentrolls and Hisenverts ordered by the Forschungsfuhrung des Reichsministers der Luftfahrt und Oberbefehlshabers der Luftwaffe in 1942 and 1943.

B) Theoretical and practical work involved.

C) Dipl. Ing. Kober, Dipl. Ing. Hermann, Ing. Buchmann.

D) Coils for establishing homogeneous a.c. fields for testing purposes. 50 c/s multistage valvevoltmeter. Compensating arrangement for a.c. Additional equipment for normal magnetic measurements. Nothing was evacuated from Wolfersdorf.

E) An exceptional high degree of shielding was required for the storage coil of hisentrolls. (See project 39). The remaining field should be less than 1% of the original fieldstrength. The use of alloys with high permeability gave rise to new trouble caused by fluttering of the thin sheets of the shields. So we came back to thick circular shielding boxes of soft iron annealed after the manufacture. Some viewpoints were found out and approved by tests which would enable the design of such shields with elementary analytical methods based upon the properties of the material.

F) Theoretical considerations completed; should not the results of the tests still to come give rise to new ideas? Tests advanced, through not completed as an annealing furnace of sufficient volume was not available. I should think it advisable to carry the work further on the same lines as before.

G) Not completed. A provisional report as to the methods employed and the results obtained can be prepared, using the notes of the associates. No final paper available without further experimental work.

Project 20

Stray Field of Transformers and Iron Cored Coils

A) This project was not covered by a special order of any agency, though it is to a certain extent connected to the design of Hisentrolls and Hisenverts ordered by the Forschungsfuhrung des Reichsministers der Luftfahrt und Oberbefehlshabers der Luftwaffe. It was investigated in 1942.

B) Mainly experimental work according to a general theoretical conceipt.

C) Dipl. Ing. Schrader, cand. el. Todt.

D) Equipment similar to that used in connection with project 19. Not evacuated from Wolfersdorf.

E) The general idea was to look at the stray field or iron cored windings as magnetic dipoles of a definite moment with a definite axis. The quality of any such apparatus could be defined by indicating the magnetic moment. The indication or the direction of this moment would be a valuable help for the engineer who is to design apparatus with iron cored windings as accessories. This aspect was well approved by the tests even for nearby distances. The theory has shown the way for evaluating the moment to be expected from the dimensions, type and material of the transformer or coil.

F) Experimental work completed. Approval on a larger scale desirable but not necessary. Theoretical considerations completed. Work has been dropped since the end of 1942 on account of other more urgent projects.

G) No report has been established as yet. A final paper can be prepared using the information laid down in the personal files of the associates.

Project 21.

Modulation of C.W. Short Wave Transmission in the Propagation Way

(Codename: Fernlauschgerat 39)

A) This project was suggested by the Heereswaffenamt WaPruf 7 in 1938.

B) Practical and theoretical work involved.

C) Dr. Zech.

D) Special transmitter in the 6 m band. Special receiver. Directional aerials. Special microphones. The equipment has in entirety been delivered to the Heereswaffenamt in 1942. No equipment could therefore be evacuated from Wolfersdorf.

E) It was intended for secret supervising purposes to have a c.w. transmission of high-frequency energy modulated at a place remote from the transmitter by means of speech picked up by a microphone without any power supply to the modulating spot. Carbon-mikes were found superior to any other type for this purpose. They were inserted in the middle of a dipole antenna tuned to the 50 Mc/s transmitter modulating the reflective properties with the fluctuations of resistance due to speech. The direct signal from the transmitter to the receiving aerial was removed by a de-coupling arrangement of both aerials and by a compensation set adjustable in amplitude and phase. Thus the modulation amplitude of the received tension was sufficient to guarantee understandable modulation for a distance range of about 100 yards.

F) The project was entirely completed in 1942. The equipment was handed to the Heereswaffenamt after final tests carried out in Danzig in the presence of engineers of Wapruf 7, who approved the requirements to be met. Observations gathered during these tests gave rise to the idea investigated as project 22 later on.

G) Description of the equipment and regulations for practical use have been sent to the Heereswaffenamt. A scientific paper on the subject covered has been presented by Dr. Zech to the Electrical Department of the Technische Hochschule Danzig as a dissertation. No copy being found in Wolfersdorf, it could not be evacuated from there.

Project 22.

C.W. Short Wave RADAR

(Codename: Luchs)

A) This project originated from occasional observations in connection with project 21. in 1942. After a first order given by the Department GL-CH 4 of the Reichsluftfahrtminister; the work was finally done under the aegis of the Forschungsfuhrung des Reichsministers der Luftfahrt und Oberbefehlshabers der Luftwaffe.

B) Practical and theoretical work involved.

C) Dr. V. Rautenfeld, Dipl. Ing. Kroeker, Dipl. Ing. Latz, Dipl. Ing. Leistner.

D) Luchs-Equipment in various designs. The last design was evacuated from Wolfersdorf. Various transmitters, aerials, receivers, output meters, valvevoltmeters and so on. Nothing of these parts was evacuated from Wolfersdorf, part of the equipment is probably in Travemunde.

E) The main idea for this project was to use a frequency equal to or near to the fundamental frequency of the plane itself in order to have a high level of the reflected signal. The balance between the input of the receiving antenna loop caused by normal coupling to the transmitting dipole aerial and a compensating tension derived from the output circuit of the transmitter is upset by the presence of the plane operating as a powerful reflector. The distance range of the equipment is given by the limits set by the possible values of the equilibrium of the compensation, i.e. the compensating quality. It was shown by the experiments, that the distance range is practically limited to 1 to 2 miles, though the mechanical design of the compensating elements would allow for qualities as high as 1 to a million. The causes for such trouble are discussed.

F) All parts of the equipment were brought into operating conditions. Tests were carried out on the ground as well as aboard aircraft. Practical experience could be fully explained by theoretical considerations. The knowledge gathered led to the projects 23 to 25.

G) The equipment was completed in the beginning of 1944. The observations were finally discussed at the end of 1944. A paper has been presented by Prof. Schwenkhagen to the Funkmesskommission in March 1944. The main investigator presented two papers covering the whole experience and theory. The first of these papers was evacuated from Wolfersdorf and listed in Wiesbaden as Y6. The second one was not found.

Project 23.

Short Wave Proximity Fuse

(Codename: Pinscher)

A) The project sprang from our investigations regarding project 22. Formal order was given by the Forschungsfuhrung des Reichsministers der Luftfahrt und Oberbefehlshabers der Luftwaffe in 1944.

B) Practical and theoretical work involved.

C) Dr.V.Rautenfeld, Dipl. Ing. Leistner, Dipl. Ing. Latz.

D) Some devices for testing purposes and as models for future manufacture have been made by us and by the Reichsrundfunkgesellschaft (National Broadcasting Company). For testing purposes a moving coil oscillograph and camera equipment with electric release was used. All of this equipment was left in Travemunde; it could therefore not be evacuated from Wolfersdorf.

E) As for project 22 the main idea was to make use of the fundamental frequency of the plane to be attacked for the transmitter and receiver of the device, thus establishing a high reflective power of the target. In fact, some volts were found as useful signal reflected by the target across the resonant circuit of the receiver aerial with about 2 watts radiation energy of the transmitter. Thus very simple schemes could be used with normal valves, one for the transmitter, a second one for the receiver. The fluctuations of the place current of the receiver tube caused the fuse to operate. With a differentiating device inserted in the place circuit all compensating equipment - such as described in connection with project 22 - could be disposed of. Flight tests with the fuse arranged on the ground gave evidence of satisfactory operation and showed a distance range up to about 50 yards.

F) All data necessary for the final design of the device have been afforded. Development for practical use could be started at once. Flight tests have shown sufficient sensitivity as well as reliability. Further tests are desirable to give proof of the behaviour of the device when moving with the projectile.

G) The remarks given above in paragraph F indicate the state of our research at the end of March. A provisional report was about to be written by the main investigator, who probably is still in Travemunde. No information regarding this subject was found in Wolfersdorf.

Project 24

Remote Controlled Short Wave Proximity Fuse

(Codename: Marder)

A) Work on this project was done following directions given by the "Sonderkommission fur Zunderfragen des Reichsministers fur Rustung und Kriegsproduktion (SKfZ)" with the approval of the Bevollmachtigter der Hochfrequenzforschung BHF. It was started in summer 1944.

B) Practical and theoretical work involved.

C) Dr. Ing. v. Rautenfeld, Dipl. Ing. Kroeker.

D) One valve transmitter in various designs. Special receiver with frequency metering arrangement in the output. Electrically controlled camera and moving coil oscillograph. All of this equipment being left in Travemunde in order to push the work, no equipment could be found in Wolfersdorf.

E) The frequency of a transmitter determined by the data of the antenna circuit is shifted on approach of a target due to its acting as a reflector and changing the reactive load of the antenna circuit. The fluctuation of frequency is picked up in a receiver aboard the fighter or on the ground. Sudden change of the frequency is to operate the transmission of a special command via a wireless channel normally used for the remote control of the movements of the projectile causing the fuse to blow up the charge. In our mind this method should have been less liable to premature fusing or jamming by enemy countermeasures than other projects were. Tests have been carried out with the fuse arranged on the ground to control an automatic camera equipment; they have been successful. The distance range for the fuse was about 50 yards, for the distance of projectile and commanding post no difficulties were realized up to 10 miles.

F) Provisional tests with laboratory type equipment had successfully been carried out in January 1945. Further tests with regard to the behaviour of the device under flight conditions and its liability to be affected by enemy action should be executed, if the method is taken into consideration. The main advantage over other systems is due to the utmost simplicity of the device inside the projectile; 1 tube of any type available, 1 antenna of small dimensions, small amount of supply energy needed

G) Not completed. The main investigator would be able to give a report of the stage reached. Final judgement and report cannot be given before further testing has been done.

Project 25

Improved Short Wave Proximity Fuse

(Codename: Wiesel)

A) This work was started in 1944 in order to fulfil requirements set forth by the Sonderkommission fur Zunderfragen (SKfZ) des Reichsministers fur Rustung und Kriegsproduktion in agreement with the Bevollmachtigter fur Hochfrequenzforschung (BHF).

B) Practical and theoretical work involved.

C) Dr.v. Rautenfeld, Dipl. Ing. Latz, Ing. Bierenbrodt.

D) Various designs of fuse equipment, moving coil oscillograph, electrically operated camera. All of this equipment being used in Travemunde no parts could be found in Wolfersdorf.

E) An important drawback involved in the Pinscher-fuse (see project 23) was the need for two antennae and two valves. The Wiesel-Fuse was to use but one antenna and one tube. Again as with the Marder device (see project 24) the target was to influence the loading of the transmitter by the fluctuations of the radiation resistance of the aerial used as the main oscillating circuit of the generator tube, whether such fluctuations should happen to be resistive or reactive. In each case the oscillating conditions of the tube are changed giving rise to fluctuations of the d.c. working conditions of the tube, e.g. the d.c. plate current. These fluctuations were to operate the fuse... of course, the fundamental frequency of the target was to be used in the same way as in connection with the other projects mentioned.

F) Test equipment was completed and tested by flying over it when arranged on the ground. Results were satisfactory. Final design for flight tests could be started. It was intended to investigate the question of which frequencies should be most advantageous for such type of fuse, the same principle being proposed by others for different frequency-ranges, (Fox-AEG and Kugelblitz-PVG Salzburg) and what properties are most desirable for the tubes used in the transmitter. The laboratory was awaiting a formal order for such additional research.

G) Not completed. A provisional report might be given by the main associate in charge of the investigations. No final report possible without further experimental work.

Project 26

Measuring Current and Tension Distribution in Oscillating Bodies

A) This project was started by our laboratory in connection with the tests necessary for the projects 22 to 25. No special order from any agency was given for these tests.

B) Experimental as well as theoretical work involved.

C) Dipl. Ing. Latz.

D) 2 or 3 current metering calibrated devices; 2 or 3 tension and high frequency fieldstrength metering devices. All of this equipment was needed for the testing done for the projects 23 to 25 in Travemunde. Thus nothing could be found in Wolfersdorf. Order having been given to move the plane with some of the devices installed to Altenburg in Eastern Thuringia these parts perhaps might be picked up there, otherwise they should still be in Travemunde.

E) In connection with the projects 22 to 25 the radial distribution of radiated power around a plane acting as an oscillator was investigated. In order to account for the characteristics found the distribution of current over the surface of the wings and the fuselage was to be known. The work done for this project made provision for the necessary metering equipment, using one-wire-loops as pick-ups for the magnetic field due to the current and small sheet antennas as pick-ups for the electric fieldstrength near the surface of the plane. Special attention was paid to thoroughly discoupling the ammeter from influences of the electric field and vice versa.

F) All of the devices mentioned above in paragraph D were completed and used for laboratory measurements after calibration since 1943 to 1944. No further work to be done.

G) A paper covering the subject of this project was under preparation by the investigator.

Project 27.

Fundamental Wavelength of Planes and their Quality

A) This project was raised in connection with our investigations relating to projects 22 to 25 using the equipment designed under project 26. No special order was given by any agency. The work was started in 1943.

B) Practical and theoretical work involved.

C) Dr. v. Rautenfeld, Dipl. Ing. Latz, Dipl. Ing. Stange.

D) Metering devices mentioned in connection with project 26. Planes with special installations and connections for using them as test-objects. (W 34b and Do 17Z). The planes were ordered to Altenburg in the beginning of April 1945. They were not reported to have arrived there. They might either be found in Altenburg (Thuringia) or in Travemunde.

E) In order to enable the proper choice of wavelength for the proximity fuses dealt with in the projects 23 to 25, information relating to the fundamental frequency, the distribution of radiated power and the quality of the plane acting as a transmitting antenna was urgently needed. Under this project the necessary data was obtained. The difference between the properties on the ground and during flight were recognised. We had in mind to compare the results of the tests with the values evaluated by analytical methods from the dimensions of the plane using as elementary analysis as possible. Apparently, we were very close to this goal.

F) Experimental work was done for two different types of plane. A third one was still to be tested. Theoretical considerations were approaching completion. As yet no paper with a description of the results is available. The investigators should have all necessary information in their files to complete such report.

Project 28.

Atmospheric Radiation as a Source of Trouble for Long Wave Infra-Red

(Codename: Butterblume)

A) This project was suggested by the Forschungsfuhrung des Reichsministers der Luftfahrt and Oberbefehlshabers der Luftwaffe in 1942. Later on the Department GL-Flak of the same ministry and the Oberkommando der Kriegsmarine gave additional orders for the same object.

B) Gathering of experimental data. Theoretical work was merely done for evaluation of the tests.

C) Dipl.Ing.Schmude, Dipl.Ing.Hermann, Dipl.Ing.Ribbeck, Ing. Bierenbrodt.

D) Thermoelement with rotatable parabolic mirror, set of filters, hisentroll of ultimate sensitivity, recording equipment. All of this was picked up in Sonneberg and listed at T-Branch G-2 in Wiesbaden as E1 to 15. Infrared spectrograph for wavelengths down to 10μ was evacuated from Wolfersdorf and listed in Wiesbaden as F 1.

E) For all kind of infrared equipment the main difficulties arise from disturbing radiation of the Background, i.e. emitted from the atmosphere. Tests carried out in Danzig during 1943 and 1944 showed the level of the fluctuations of such radiation even during nighttime to be highly above the sensitivity available when using a thermoelement together with a hisentroll. The radiated energy of planes was measured with the same equipment. Records were to be continued with an improved recording equipment fitted with infrared filters in order to recognise the distribution of radiated energy to the range of wavelength. The infrared spectrograph was to serve the same purpose.

F) Sufficient recording had been done to allow for a general view of the project. The new equipment for spectral analysis of the radiation by means of filters was completed and installed in Sonneberg. First results were available. For their interpretation theoretical work was still to be done. The infrared spectrograph was completed, but not calibrated. Surprising knowledge had been gained relating to invisible haloes of the sun apparently due to some kind of aerosol.

G) Two reports summarizing in an abridged form the results of our Danzig records had been prepared by our laboratory and had been sent to the Forschungsfuhrung of the Reichsluftfahrtministerium as well as to GL-Flak and to other interested people. No further copy of these papers was found in Wolfersdorf. Further investigation of the spectral distribution of infrared radiation and the halophenomena observed in our prior tests would be of general interest in our mind disregarding all military applicances.

Project 29

Highly sensitive Thermoelements for Radiation Metering with Short Time Lag

(Codename: Butterblume)

A) This project was started in connection with the investigations relating to project 28 and 30-31 without a special order given from any agency, because we were recognising that none of the thermoelements then on the market met our requirements.

B) Practical technological work.

C) Dipl. Ing. Schude, Mr. Rennack.

D) Thermoelements of various design for various purposes. Some samples of such elements together with material for preparing other ones were evacuated from Wolfersdorf. See list of T-Branch G-2 under F 10-11. Short time metering set for determining time constants of elements was evacuated too (See list F9) Vacuum equipment with high tension d.c. supply for electrode cleaning by glow discharge and high current transformer for evaporization purposes with power pack and switchboard, furnace with automatic electric temperature control, small annealing oven, black body for calibration were as yet not removed from Wolfersdorf.

E) A Modern technology for preparing thermoelements of sturdy construction not subject to aging with high sensitivity and small mass to arrive at low time constants was developed. An extremely thin glass foil melted upon a calite ring was used as a support for the thermo-couple which was deposited thereon by evaporization under vacuum conditions. Normally bismuth and antimony (pure) were used as thermomaterials reinforcing the connections with silver and copper. After installing shields and blacking the receiving surface with a carbon coating the element was included in a glass-housing with a normal valve socket at the lower end and shut by a vacuum tight KRS 5 place cover at the upper end. The sensitivity and time constant of the elements were tested; of course they depend upon the thickness of the metal foils as well as on the vacuum used.

F) The technology was fully developed. A man skilled in the art was able to prepare even very complicated arrangements of elements such as wanted for instance for project 31 with a high degree of accuracy.

G) Thermoelements have as well been made for our own purposes as for other laboratories and agencies. Thermoelements designed by Prof. Dr. Monch using tellurium as one of the metals were tested by us in collaboration with Prof. Monch with regard to sensitivity and time constant. Neither a scientific paper presenting the results reached with our design, nor written regulations for the make of the elements do exist at the time being.

Project 30

Infra-Red Mapping Equipment

(Codename: Butterblume)

A) This project was started as part of the general project suggested by the Forschungsfuhrung des Reichsministers der Lufthahrt und Obserbefehlshabers der Luftwaffe with regard to our infrared investigations. See project 28. It was started when the success in the design of thermoelements together with the hisentroll rendered possible some kind of infrared television with coarse scanning and low sequence of pictures.

B) Mainly practical work involved.

C) Dipl. Ing. Schmude, Ing. Bierenbrodt.

D) Multiple thermoelement, rotating multistage switching device with motor drive, special type of hisenvert, indicator cathode ray tube. These parts have been evacuated from Wolfersdorf and are listed in T-Branch G-2 as F7 and F8. The camera equipment for fixing the image appearing on the screen, the parabolic mirror for the pick-up and the recent design of an electrolytic recorder for the map have not been found. They may probably be among the rest of the laboratory's equipment stored in Eckernforde or in Travemunde.

E) A line of ten equally sensitive thermoelements (see project 29) mounted in the focal plane of a parabolic mirror is consecutively connected to the storage coil of a special hisenvert by means of a rotating switch which at the same time operates the sweep of the electron beam in a horizontal direction. The intensity of brightness of the spot is controlled by the amplitude of the peaks arising when the circuit of the storage coil is broken by the switch. The equipment is to be installed with a vertical axis into the floor of the fuselage of a plane. The infrared picture of the ground flown over is fixed by photographing the screen of the cathode ray tube on a film, the speed of which is set according to the height of flight and the velocity of the plane. In order to have the map appearing in visible form without developing the film in a darkroom an electrolytical recorder took the place of the cathode ray tube in a recent form of the device.

F) The mapping equipment was entirely completed. Images of models with low temperature radiation such as human bodies for instance had successfully been taken, though they do not show such details on account of the coarse scanning. Flight tests with the photographic recorder succeeded in taking maps of areas near Danzig in fair agreement with normal maps.

G) The equipment was completed in autumn 1944, the electrolytic recorder however, not before the beginning of 1945. An abridge version of the results with a number of photographic records included was given by Mr. Schmude and sent to the Heereswaffenamt WaPruf 8. They were to copy it and send it to other interested people. No such copy was received until April 15th.

Project 31

Infra Red Aiming Equipment

(Codename: Butterblume)

A) This project was started in 1944 when the Forschungsfuhrung des Reichsministers der Luftfahrt und Oberbefehlshabers der Luftwaffe feared that short wave infra red equipment for night-fighting might fail on account of the possibility of shielding the outlets of the engines to temperatures below 180°F.

B) Mainly practical work involved.

C) Dipl. Ing. Schmude, Ing. Bierenbrodt.

D) Multiple thermoelement, rotating multistage switching device with motor drive, special type of hisenvert, indicator cathode ray tube. These parts have been evacuated from Wolfersdorf and listed at T-3 Branch G-2 in Wiesbaden as F 3 to 5. To accomplish the assembly for practical use nothing would be needed but an additional mirror of some 12" diameter.

E) The equipment is very similar to that described in project 30. The main difference is the arrangement of the thermoelement. It consists in a central element of small dimensions exactly focussed for fine aiming surrounded by 8 larger elements slightly defocussed. These 9 elements are consecutively connected to the storage coil of the hisenvert by means of the rotating switch, deflecting at the same time the spot of the cathode ray oscillograph to respective points on the screen. The brightness of the spot is again controlled by the peaks of the hisenvert. To account for the average brightness of the background 8 further elements connected in parallel are arranged in the space between each two of the 8 elements mentioned above and inserted in series into the main circuit.

F) The equipment was completed. First tests on the ground had been carried out with a fist used as target. It was possible to locate it with sufficient accuracy within a range of 30 yards. It was concluded that the accuracy for aiming at a plane would be sufficient for all distances required by the military authorities. Further tests would have to be carried out under flight conditions to give evidence of the reliability of the equipment and of the suitability to real targets.

G) Device completely ready for test purposes. No report or regulations for practical use as yet available.

Project 32.

Thermoelectric Detector as a Standard for very high frequencies

A) This project was suggested by the Bevollmachtigter der Hochfrequenzforschung (BHF) in summer 1944. An official order was still pending.

B) Mainly practical work involved.

C) Dipl. Ing. Schmude, Dipl. Ing. Leider, Dipl. Ing. Schrader.

D) First model of thermoelectric dipole detectorstandard for 3000 Mc/s. This model was not found in Wolfersdorf.

E) The results obtained with radiation metering thermoelements and hisentrolls or hisenverts (see projects 29, 39 to 43) raised the idea of using thermoelements as high frequency detectors for hyperfrequency too. The technology developed in our laboratory would allow for the design of electric dipoles as well as small loop antennas tuned for the frequency at which measurements were to be done, in the form of thermoelements matched in resistance to the radiating resistance of the dipole. According to preliminary evaluation the sensitivity should be of the same order as is hitherto afforded with crystal detectors. Though inferior to the crystal detector with regard to time constant, the thermoelectric detector should be preferred as a standard for c.w. hyperfrequency on account of the stability of response that can be expected and the sturdiness of mechanical design.

F) The project was just about to be started in the beginning of April 1945, after our investigations regarding the projects 29 and 39 to 43 had almost been completed for the first instance. Technological work as well as testing of the properties of the standards to be developed would be necessary.

G) Since the work was in the very beginning, no report is available.

Project 33.

Characteristics of Detectors for very high frequencies

A) This project as part of the general measuring program of the laboratory in the high frequency field without a special order given by any authority was started in the end of 1944.

B) Mainly theoretically; some additional tests to prove the accuracy of theoretical deductions.

C) Dipl. Ing. Leider.

D) Measuring lines for different ranges of frequency. None of these lines was evacuated from Wolfersdorf.

E) In order to evade the need of a calibrated potentiometer almost impossible for hyperfrequency the distribution of tension along a measuring line shortcircuited or not loaded at the end may be used as a standard for examining the dependency of the response of detecting devices on the amplitude of the tension to be measured. The project was to deal with the deviations to be expected from sinusoidal distribution due to damping of the line, loading caused by the resistive and reactive properties of the detector tube calibrated and with the influence of matching conditions of the source of hyperfrequency energy to the line.

F) Theoretical considerations mainly completed. Tests for wavelengths of 1.5 m accomplished. Tests for wavelengths in the dm-range and with waveguides in the cm range under consideration.

G) A paper presenting our recent knowledge had been written by the investigator and was handed to the BHF in the beginning of 1945. No copy was found in Wolfersdorf.

Project 34

Contact Potential

A) This project was started on our own behalf in connection with the projects 35 and 9, which were done according to orders given by the Forschungsfuhrung des Reichsministers der Luftfahrt und Oberbefehlshabers der Luftwaffe. First tests were carried out in 1943.

B) Experimental work almost exclusively.

C) Dipl. Ing. Pohl.

D) Electrodynamic vibrators of various design, beat frequency oscillator with special amplifier, pick-up equipment, compensating box and special amplifier for zero indication. Except the beat frequency oscillator the equipment was evacuated from Wolfersdorf. It is specified in the list of T-Branch G-2 in Qiesbaden as B 1 to 7.

E) Trouble experienced with generating voltmeters of high sensitivity suggested the idea that the contact potential of a metal plate was not constant all over the surface. A preliminary investigation by means of a new method for measuring small electrostatic voltages with high accuracy revealed differences in contact potential as high as 0.5 volts for the same sheet of metal. Platinum offered the larges fluctuations, whereas bismuth was found to have the smallest differences. A definite influence of moisture was established. Tests under vacuum conditions were considered.

F) A considerable amount of experience with the techniques of these measurements has been gathered. Effects of external field strength to the contact potential made us think of relations existing between these measurements and the rectifying process in or near the surface of a crystal detector. Additional tests under various conditions of the surface and its surroundings especially under vacuum would be of great interest from any point of scientific view.

G) Not completed. Some preliminary notes on the subject have been sent to the BHF. No information in written form was evacuated from Wolfersdorf. The investigator might be able to give a preliminary report of our results and hypotheses relying upon his personal notes.

Project 35.

Generating Voltmeters
(Codename: Feldmuhle)

A) This project was begun in 1938 with financial help granted by the "Forschungsgemeinschaft der Deutschen Wissenschaft". Later on the Forschungsfuhrung des Reichsministers der Luftfahrt und Oberbefehlshaber der Luftwaffe took interest in it in connection with our investigations relating to atmospheric electricity and atmospherics (see projects 8 to 14).

B) Experimental work almost exclusively.

C) Dipl. Ing. Rangs, Dipl. Ing. Pohl.

D) Generating voltmeters for normal use on the ground and for use aboard aircraft. Special amplifiers for these voltmeters and recording equipment for the output. The parts evacuated from Wolfersdorf were entered into the list of T-Branch G-2 in Wiesbaden as G1 to 8.

E) The principle of the generating voltmeter - for the first time suggested and used by the referee in 1925 - had later on been improved by American and Japanese scientists by the use of amplifying devices for the output of the electrostatic generator itself. This however included the drawback, that the final output was dependent on the amplification factor of the amplifier and that the sign of the measured fieldstrength or tension was lost. We proposed to overcome these difficulties by adding an electromagnetic generator coupled to the same axis. Its voltage is connected in series to the electrostatic voltage which is periodically short circuited by a switch operated by a clock. Thus a standard voltage is introduced into the record allowing for the estimate of all external influences to the results. Moreover the sign of the primary tension is always well known, depending upon the fact whether the output is increased or decreased upon the short circuiting of the electrostatic generator.

F) The design of the device with a lowest range of $200 \mu v/m$ has been completed. Some apparatus have been delivered to other investigators such as the Reichsamt fur Wetterdienst and the Deutsche Versuchsanstalt fur Segelflug. (National Bureau for Weather and National Research Laboratory for Gliding). Some devices were continuously used in our own projects. Trouble has been experienced with the aircraft type on account of difficulties with the d.c. motors.

G) A full report of the design used and all difficulties encountered has been given by the first investigator, Dipl. Ing. Rangs:

"Device for Measuring the Atmospheric Fieldstrength"

It was published about 2 years ago. A copy was evacuated from Wolfersdorf listed under D14 in Wiesbaden at T-Branch G-2. Another paper covering the same subject was published in the "Elektrizitatswirtschaft" by Prof. Dr. Schwenkhagen.

Project 36.

Pulse Transformers

A) This project was suggested by the Bevollmachtigter der Hochfrequenzforschung (BHF) in 1944.

B) Gathering of information from different laboratories and factories. Report of a meeting held on the subject under the direction of Prof. Schwenkhagen. Merely theoretical work.

C) Dipl. Ing. Roewer.

D) No special equipment.

E) For Radar, television and similar equipment there was a broad field for pulse transformers up to very high voltages and power. This project was to make provision for general rules for the design of such transformers with the final goal to establish some standard types for normal working conditions. The work was divided as follows: Deformation of pulses due to transformer design and properties, magnetic material and design of core, dielectric strength and design of winding, internal capacity, losses and cooling system, accessories, such as bushings, case, expansion vessel or similar devices, special requirements for flight conditions.

F) The indications given above in paragraph E are a program. Only parts of it were under investigation. Orders had been given requesting other laboratories to carry out special tests in order to get the necessary information in full detail. Almost nothing has been seen in Wolfersdorf and in Travemunde after the evacuation from Danzig. Perhaps the material gathered by the investigator is still in one of the crates in Eckernforde. Establishing of such general rules would in our mind be desirable for comercial use of pulse transformers.

G) No report as yet available. General lines might be fixed by the investigator based upon his own notes.

Project 37.

Charging line, Pulse transformer and Valve Load

A) This project was suggested by the Bevollmachtigter der Hochfrequenzforschung (BHF) early in 1945.

B) Mainly theoretical work to account for existing experimental experience.

C) Prof. Dr. Quade, Mr. Keskula.

D) No special equipment used.

E) The deformation of the pulse, which would be delivered by the charging line to a Ohmic resistance, due to the interposition of a pulse transformator of know properties and to the influence of the different types of tubes connected to its secondary and changing with oscillating conditions during the pulse period is a highly interesting mathematical problem. This is especially true for very short waves, when the transformer cannot be considered as a static device, but must be taken into consideration with the properties determining its behaviour to transients. It was intended to investigate all of these questions from a merely theoretical standpoint with a view to finding out the reasons for some trouble experienced in practical design.

F) Prof. Quade who was to be in charge of this project had only joined the laboratory in January 1945. No work had as yet been done except some general discussions of the subject.

G) No report available.

Project 38.

Pulse Analyser

A) There was no special order given for this project by any agency. The work was done in connection with our investigations relating to measurements in the hyperfrequency field. (See project 4). It was started in 1944.

B) Experimental and theoretical work involved.

C) Pulse analysing set with power pack. Not evacuated from Wolfersdorf. The device was under construction in Travemunde and should have been completed there in the meantime.

D) Dipl. Ing. Hollmann. Ing. Vesper.

E) Pulses may as well be described by the shape of a single pulse as given in an oscillogramm, as by the spectrum of side frequencies connected to the carrier of pulse modulated high frequency. This project was to deal with the second aspect confined to the r.m.s. amplitude of the spectrum notwithstanding the phase conditions of the various frequencies. A wobbled auxiliary frequency is superimposed to the pulse modulated signal. The output of the intermediate frequency is connected to the vertical plates of a cathode ray oscillograph, while the horizontal sweep is simultaneously influenced by the auxiliary frequency to account for a linear abscissa gauge. The general lines of the equipment are very similar to a prior design of Telefunken.

F) When we left Danzig, the device was almost completed. It should in the meantime have entirely been completed in Travemunde, where the investigators had been left until the beginning of April 1945. No tests with the device have however been executed.

G) As yet no reports available. The main investigator should be able to present a paper referring to the working principles of the device in full detail as well as regulations for the practical use of the apparatus.

Project 39.

Highly Sensitive D.C. Controlling Device. (HISENTROLL)

(Codename: Steuerumformer)

A) This project was originated by the referee early in 1939 without an order of any agency. After the main results had been obtained the Forschungsfuhrung des Reichsministers der Luftfahrt und Oberbefehlshabers der Luftwaffe was given a report. They at once gave order for further investigation in 1942 and for the design of a score of apparatus.

B) Experimental and theoretical work involved. Development, too, has been done for the device considered.

C) Dipl. Ing. Schrader, Dipl. Ing. Schmidt, Ing. Buchmann.

D) Hereunder a number added to the word Hisentroll always indicates the sensitivity of the device. It is the reversed power of 10 in watts necessary to operate the output pulses of the device. Hisentroll 11 or d.c. supply. This type has been delivered to AEG. This firm was a licensee for the Hisentroll patents. Hisentroll 11 for a.c. supply. 5 devices were evacuated from Wolfersdorf and listed A1 and A3a to 3d in Wiesbaden at T-Branch G-2. Hisentroll 15 for a.c. supply. 2 Devices were evacuated from Wolfersdorf and listed A4 and 5 in Wiesbaden. Hisentrolls 17 were under design. Not evacuated. All further equipment belonging to this project was not evacuated. Input generators, testing equipment for the chopping breaker, cathode ray oscillographs, compensating boxes, various shieldings for storage coils, various types of storage coils.

E) The Hisentrolls is a relay as sensitive as a galvanometer, but unaffected by mechanical vibration and the like. The input circuit consists of a coil in series with a breaker. When the breaker suddenly opens its contacts, the energy stored in the magnetic field of the coil gives rise to transients oscillations of the tension across the coil. These tensions are wither immediately or after amplification applied to the grid of a gas-filled triode (thyratron), the plate of which is connected to the a.c. supply. The peak of the transient ignites the discharge of the triode, allowing a flow of plate current until the next zero value occurs. Opening of the breaker and flow of anode current, as long as the peak is high enough, are repeated at 50 c/s.

F) The fundamental theory for the device including the question of appropriate matching is accomplished. Devices for the type 11 have been designed and delivered to other laboratories. The development for type 15 was completed, all drawings for manufacture were prepared. Making a score of apparatus of this type was considered by the BHF. For even higher sensitivity see project 42.

G) But for special questions such as the best form of shielding the storage coil (see project 19), contact material and mechanical design of a cheap, but reliable breaker, use of a less expensive type of thyratron, the project was completed. The results are summarized in a paper presented by Prof. Schwenkhagen:

The HISENTROLL

a copy of which was evacuated from Wolfersdorf. (T-Branch G-2 list number A2a and b). The drawings for the more recent design of the Hisentroll 15 were not evacuated from Wolfersdorf. Further reports relating to more recent experience are referred to with project 42.

Project 40.

Highly sensitive D.C. Measuring Converter. Hisenvert

Codename: Messwertumformer)

A) This project is strongly correlated to the Hisentroll project 39. After the first F was presented, the Forschungsfuhrung des Reichsministers der Luftfahrt und Oberbefehlshabers der Luftwaffe took interest in the project, giving order to manufacture a score of such devices which were to be distributed to various laboratories. This order was given in the beginning of 1944.

B) Mainly practical work involved, the theory being given in connection with project 39.

C) Dipl. Ing. Schmude. Ing. Bierenbrodt, Dipl. Ing. Schmidt.

D) The figure added to the word Hisenvert hereunder indicates the sensitivity of the device in watts in inversed powers of 10. Hisenverts 15. Normal design manufactured by a factory in Berlin with the consent of the AEG, who hold the license for these devices. 6 apparatus of this type were evacuated from Wolfersdorf. They are listed as A7 to f at T-Branch G-2 in Wiesbaden. Two further devices of type 15, but of special design listed as A2 and A9 were evacuated, together with one hisenvert of type 16 (A10). Other additional equipment similar to that mentioned in connection with project 39 was not evacuated.

E) The main principle of the Hisenvert is equal to that of the Hisentroll (See project 39). The transient across the storage coil of the input circuit is, however, not used to ignite a thyratron, but the peaks are measured by means of a valve (electronic) voltmeter. The plate current of the last stage tube is within a certain range almost proportionate to the input tension. Repeated calibration can however not be disposed of. In order to allow measuring of tensions of both signs provision is made for entering an additional small d.c. voltage, tapped from a fixed resistance into the input circuit. Whereas the Hisenvert may be looked at as a somewhat nonlinear d.c. amplifier with regard to the output current, the current fed to the resistance mentioned above is exactly proportionate to the input tension, if the device is compensated by hand to a fixed output.

F) The fundamental principle is laid open in connection with project 39. The design of the hisenvert 15 is completed, though not satisfactory, on account of a too narrow assembly of power pack and metering element. An improved design is desirable. For the sake of elevated sensitivity reference is made to project 42.

G) The general lines of the Hisenvert are reported in the paper already mentioned in connection with project 39.

The HISENTROLL

which was presented by Prof. Schwenkhagen. Two copies of this paper were evacuated from Wolfersdorf. They are listed as A 2a and A 2b in Wiesbaden at T-Branch G-2.

Project 41.

Self-balanced Hisentrolls as linear D.C. Amplifiers

A) This project was started in connection with the order of the Forschungsfuhrung des Reichsministers der Luftfahrt und Oberbefehlshabers der Luftwaffe in 1942, though the idea had already been conceived prior to this date, when the first results with the Hisentroll had been achieved in 1939.

B) Experimental work together with some theoretical considerations.

C) Dipl. Ing. Schrader, Dipl. Ing. Schmidt, Ing. Buchmann.

D) On the lines fixed by the laboratory a score of feed back devices with automatic setting was manufactured by the Siemens factory in Danzig. 6 apparatus of this type to be used with Hisentrolls 11 and 15 (see project 39) were picked up in Wolfersdorf and listed in Wiesbaden at T-Branch G-2 under A 6a to A 6f. One more sample of prior make was evacuated from Weida and listed A 1a. Further samples are still available in Wolfersdorf.

E) The output pulses of the Hisentroll are used to operate a small synchronous motor running in opposite direction according to the sign of the input voltage and stopping as soon as the input is reduced to zero. Geared to the motor axis a potentiometer is arranged for controlling a d.c. flowing through a resistance inserted into the input circuit of the Hisentroll, thus establishing an automatic feed-back. The d.c. mentioned will always be exactly proportionate to the input tension as soon as the zero position has been reached. Within certain limits any type of indicating or recording instrument can be inserted in the feed back circuit. Provision has been made for internal feedback in the resetting equipment in order to evade hunting. The device worked reliably up to frequencies of the input of 3 to 5 c/s. Amplification factors up to 1 up to 1,000,000,000, have been realized by way of example.

F) The device has been developed to a state which would allow for a large scale manufacture after tests to be carried out with the first series should have given proof of ordinary function. It must be emphasised that the samples evacuated from Wolfersdorf have not yet undergone any tests after the manufacture.

G) The first score of samples had come from manufacture in January 1945. Regulations for the use of the device had already been fixed in connection with prior design. There are doubts whether such regulations have been taken in Wolfersdorf or not. They might be among the papers left in Wiesbaden unclassified in one of the crates, together with records of electric field and so on.

Project 42.

Limitations of the Hisentroll.

A) In connection with some of the magnetic projects as well as with infrared measurements (see projects 15, 18 and 28), hisentrolls and hisenverts of extreme sensitivity were urgently needed. Following a suggestion of the Department FEP (Research, Development, Patent) of the Oberkommando der Kroegsmarine in 1942 this project was started. Other requirements for such devices came from different research laboratories. In 1945 we got another order from the Bevollmachtigter der Hochfrequenzforschung (BHF.)

B) Theoretical considerations coupled to simultaneous experimental work.

C) Dipl. Ing. Schmidt.

D) Laboratory design of Hisenverts 17 to 18 (see project 39) has already been in use in connection with infrared measurements (see project 28). This device has been evacuated from Sonneberg. Further experimental design existing in the laboratory was not evacuated from Wolfersdorf. The additional equipment for testing such devices, too, was not moved to Wiesbaden (Cathode ray oscillographs, Moving coil oscillogr. amplifiers, outputmeters and so on.)

E) The sensitivity of the Hisentroll and Hisenvert cannot be increased at will. Limitations are given by: Thermal noise of the resonant circuit consisting in the storage coil and its self capacity; thermal noise of the first tube of the amplifier; microphonic effect of such tube; interference from external and internal magnetic and electric fields; state of the contacts of the breaker in the input circuit. This project was to deal with these influences and to set forth the limitations given by any of these effects under various matching and service conditions. The ultimate limits for practical purposes should be in the range of 10^{-17} to 10^{-18} watts.

F) Quite a lot of experience has been gathered in the course of our investigations. To allow for a final decision very few additional tests should be sufficient. For laboratory use with careful handling and observation of all safeguards high sensitive Hisentrolls and Hisenverts are at our disposal.

G) Almost completed. The rest of work to be done mainly consists in compiling all experience gathered into a paper. The information should be in the hands of Dipl. Ing, Schmidt who was in charge of preparing such paper.

Project 43.

Vibration-Proof Hisentroll and Hisenvert

(Codename; Isegrim)

A) This project is attending project 16. The same agencies as mentioned in connection therewith are related to the work.

B) Experimental work.

C) Dipl. Ing. Kober, cand. el. Kerkovius.

D) Special type of Hisenvert (16) has been evacuated from Wolfersdorf. It was listed in Wiesbaden at T-Branch G-2 as A 1o. Moving Coil oscillograph, cathode ray oscillograph and other metering equipment used for the work has not been picked up.

E) Whereas for normal use of the Hisentroll or Hisenvert a single faulty pulse in the output would not be important, such pulse would mean premature firing in connection with project 16. Such pulses normally come from vibration, which in the case concerned, must be expected to a high extent. The present investigation was dealing with all possibilities to render a Hisentroll device entirely unaffectable by any kind of mechanical or acoustical vibration. The storage coil and its shielding, the first stage tube of the amplifying part and the vibrating chopping breaker were the parts most liable to trouble of this kind. By appropriate choice of material and design the number of faulty pulses could be removed to less than 1 in 1000 for a sensitivity of the device, that was ten times the value practically required.

F) A Hisenvert with a sensitivity of 10-16 Watt input was completed in January 1945 and has already been tested under flight conditions with full success. Further investigation of magnetic disturbances expected in connection with project 16 was under preparation.

G) Practical work completed in January 1945. As yet no paper describing the results obtained and the methods used has been prepared. The investigator can be called upon to give a report relying upon his personal notices.

Project 44.

Highly Sensitive Simple Zero-Indicating Device for High Resistance d.c. Measurements.

A) This project sprang from general work of the laboratory without any order given by any agency. After the first model had been tested the Bevollmachtigter der Hochfrequenzforschung(BHF) had in mind to have a score of such devices manufactured for distribution to other laboratories. The work was started in 1943.

B) Practical and theoretical work involved.

C) Dipl. Ing. Schmude.

D) High resistance Wheatstone bridge was evacuated from Wolfersdorf and entered into the list at T-Branch G-2 in Wiesbaden as H 2. Quasistatic voltmeter (compensation type) had been delivered to the Reichsstelle fur Hochfrequenzforschung in Ulm-Dornstadt for testing purposes and could therefore not be removed from Wolfersdorf.

E) For ultrahigh resistances, matching of the galvanometer to the bridge or other source of tension cannot be done, as long as d.c. measurements must be executed. The project removes this difficulty. Instead of the galvanometer a condenser of appropriate size is inserted in the zero circuit; This condenser is periodically discharged across a phone connected in parallel to the zero-branch. Surprisingly high accuracy can be obtained by this means even for input resistances as high as 10 to 100 Megohms. The investigation has pointed out the optimum for the elements of the wiring.

F) Work was completed since the middle of 1944. A high resistance Wheatstone bridge combined with an a.c. capacity bridge as well as a quasistatic compensating voltmeter with an input resistance of 10 Megohm were designed and made. Tests gave proof of sufficient accuracy. Development for manufacture of the device on a large scale was taken into consideration. The factory of Hartmann und Braun in Frankfurt had been contacted by us to ensure such manufacture.

G) Design and tests completed in the middle of 1944. A report was represented to the BHF in the beginning of 1945 by the investigator. No copy of this report was found in Wolfersdorf. A more complete report for publication in a technical periodical was under preparation. The investigator ought to have the necessary information for this paper.

Project 45.

Countermeasures against Homing or Remote-Controlled Torpedoe's.
(Codename: Qualle)

A) The head of the laboratory was appointed chairman of a subcommittee of the Torpedokomission des Reichsministers fur Rustung und Kreigsproduktion in the beginning of 1944.

B) Theoretical work based upon experience gathered from the reports given by the submarine-commandants and from test shootings in the Torpedo-Versuchs-Anstalt (TVA) in Gotenhafen.

C) Prof. Schwenkhagen.

D) No special equipment available in the Ernst Orlich Institut. All testing was done by the TVA.

E) The UK.IV (Subcommittee Iv) dealing with all kind of project for homing and remote-controlled torpedoes felt necessary to investigate the possibilities of enemy countermeasures against such torpedoes in order to enable a right decision as to which methods would be worth further development. Therefore, the subcommittee, under the direction of the referee, was appointed. The work related to the following types of homing or remote controlled torpedoes. Passive ultrasonic system (T5, Zaunkonig), active ultrasonic type (Geyer), Audiofrequency passive system (Taube), magnetic homing (Marchen), pressure actuated by wake (Ackermann), ultrasonic actuated by wake (Ibis), actuated by optical properties of the wake (Leuchtfisch), remote controlled by wireless channel (NY), remote controlled by means of wiring (NYK, later on known as Spinne) directional microphone headed torpedoes controlled by wiring (Lerche). For all of these types the possibilities of countermeasures by: 1) timely recognition, 2) screening, 3) deception 4) jamming, 5) destroying, including premature fusing, 6) manoeuvring were taken into careful consideration.

F) The first result was accomplished in August 1944 and presented as a report. Work was contined on the same lines after that date in order to take care of all new material relating to this question.

G) First broad report presented to the Oberkommando der Kriegsmarine by Prof. Schwenkhagen in August 1945. No copy existing of the paper except as sample sent to the OEM and on account of all information used for the report having been burnt, an excerpt of the report must be given by memory, if it is required.

PROJECT 46.

Excitation of Circular Cavity Resonators
by means of Density-modulated Beams of
Slow Electrons.

A) This work was done under an order of the Forschungsfuhrung des Reichsministers der Luftfahrt under Oberbefehlshabers der Luftwaffe. It was given some years ago about 1942 or 1943.

B) Merely theoretical work involved.

C) Dr. Steyskal.

D) Nothing.

E) The electron beam passing along the axis of a circular shaped resonant chamber exciting it by means of density modulation of the electrons in the incoming beam influences the frequencies of resonance of the chamber. In order to calculate this influence the equations for both the magnetic and the electric field in the chamber are formulated and solved. The solution is presented in the form of Bessel functions and evaluated for practical purposes, i.e. for the oscillating modes of lower orders. The work relates to infinitely thin electron beams in the first part, extending to beams of finite cross section in the second part.

F) Theoretical work completed. Experimental approval of the results might be desirable. Taking into account the influence of additional damping due to the existence of the beam in the chamber might be an interesting extension of the problem, too, as an important contribution to the design of klystrons.

G) The theoretical work is completed and laid down in a paper presented by the investigator, Dr. Steyskal:

Excitation of Circular Cavity Resonator by menas of Density-modulated Beams of slow Electrons. (2 Parts).

This paper has been evacuated from Wolfersdorf in 4 copies and has been listed under W14 and W15 (a to d for each) in Wiesbaden.

REPORT II

The following reports in German are available for inspection in the library of the Central Radio Bureau, 143 Piccadilly, W.1.

A.1. Temperature measuring equipment

Precis by Dr. Schwenkhagen of report in German No. A1 by JAKOB

Recent highly sensitive vibration proof temperature measuring equipment (JAKOB).
Compensating arrangement for tension of thermocouple with zero-indication using a chopping switch and an amplifier tuned to the chopping frequency.

A.2. The Hisentroll

Precis by Dr. Schwenhagen of report in German No. A2 by SCHWENKHAGEN.

Fundamental principle and practical design of a highly sensitive D.C. measuring and controlling device unaffected by vibration and similar disturbances. Matching and sensitivity limitations are broadly dealt with. Practical experience. Survey of possible applications, e.g. D.C. amplifier, characteristic-changer, feedback controlling equipment, etc. 10^{-18} watts limit.

A.3. Hisentroll and high resistance quas-static voltmeter

Precis by Dr. Schwenkhagen of report in German No. A3 by SCHWEIZER, PILZ.

Pages 1-6 Hisentroll (Schweizer)
Reports of tests carried out with an experimental Hisentroll set for 10^{-11} watt input. Though the Hisentroll was apparently not used in the proper way, it is stated to be a superior substitute for galvanometers in many cases. Changes in design are suggested to improve sensitivity and to render practical use more simple.

Pages 7-10 Voltmeter (Pilz)
This type of quasi-static voltmeter designed by the EO with an internal resistance of 10 M ohms is judged to be a most simple, compact and least expensive solution to the problem of measuring D.C. voltages ranging from 0.1 to 600 volts with minute current input with an accuracy of about 0.5%.

B.1. **Volta-Potentials for H₂O - Phases with meteorological interest**

Precis by Dr. Schwenkhagen of report in German No. B1 by LANGE

Experimental investigation of the Voltage-potential of the surface of single crystals of ice, of the systems : Hoarfrost-Ice Water-Ice, Metal-Water and finally Metal-Ice. The potentials found range from -o.3 to + o.5 volts. The possible influence of the presence of water and of a temperature-gradient next to the Polonium-sounding used for the measurements is broadly discussed.

25 pages with 5 figures

B.2. **On the Photoelectric Conductivity of pure Calciumsulphide**

Precis by Dr. Schwenkhagen of report in German No. B2 by FRERICHS

Experimental survey of the properties of pure Calciumsulphide, Calciumselenide and calcium telluride. The author uses single-crystals to find out the following properties: absorption-spectrum, photoelectric conductivity, extinction of photoelectric conductivity by additional infrared radiation applied, influence of temperature for some of these items. Form and design of calcium-sulphide photoresistances using synthetic single-crystals are described. Permissible load and response of such resistances for long-wave and short-wave radiation are given.

41 pages with 17 figures and 2 tables.

B.3. **Proof of Space-charge in Combined Photo-Cathodes**

Precis by Dr. Schwenkhagen of report in German No. B3 by FLEISCHER

For photoelectrodes of a more complex nature, the spectral position of the selective maximum of response has proved to be dependent upon the anode voltage.. The author is searching for the cause of such anomaly. According to his opinion it is due to the presence of space charges inside the cathode. The paper deals with special experiments to give proof of this hypothesis. He believes that the space charge layer may be of electronic nature. The relations existing between the charge and the entities responsible for its generations, namely set-up wavelength, set-up time, set-up voltage, incoming radiation level, effective surface are measured.

18 pages with 11 figures.

C.1   **Electromechanical filter equipment for damping hum**

Precis by Dr. Schwenkhagen of report in German No. C1 by FAULSTICH

A steel strip tuned to the supply frequency by varying its mechanical stress is provided with a definite small loading mass in a definite point in order to make the frequencies of its harmonics exactly coincide with the harmonics of the supply. The strip is oscillated by an exciter system. The voltage induced in a magnetic pick-up is amplified in a special amplifier and added in counterphase to the input. Thus harmonics from the third to the 20th are damped by 2-3 Np.

D.1.   Research on the Frequency Distribution of Atmospherics

Precis by Dr. Schwenkhagen of report in German No. D1 by KUROS

The distribution of atmospherics over the waveband from 200 to 3000 m investigated at two stations near Berlin. The intensity and number of armospherics decreases rapidly with decreasing wavelength.

D.2. Interference in Wireless Communications and Counter-measures to it.

Precis by Dr. Schwenkhagen of report in German No. D2 by ESAU

The author presents a survey of all kinds of interference to radio communications. It can be classified in three main types. Interference arising from other wireless transmitting systems, atmospherics and distrubances of the ionosphere and man-made statics of all kind. A summary of the general knowledge of each type of interference is given followed by a short discussion of various measures considered. Special attention is paid to the influence of interference to locating sets.

12 pages.

D.3.   Removing Static in Aircraft

Precis by Dr. Schwenkhagen of report in German No. D3 by VIEHMANN

The report is concerned with removing causes of static arising in the aircraft-equipment itself. As main sources of trouble the author discusses: 1) Static charging of the plane, 2) poor contacts changing the resistance between parts of the fuselage of the planes, 3) vibrations influencing parts of the receiver,

4) spark plugs of the motor and 5) generators, switching equipment and wiring of the main supply. Counter-measures for each source of interference are discussed including a final paragraph dealing with the possibilities offered in the design of the receiving equipment itself.

17 pages with 11 figures.

D.4. **Interference in Wireless Communication of the "Deutsche Lufthansa"**

Precis by Dr. Schwenkhagen of report in German No. D4 by STUSSEL

The paper gives additional information over that presented in D 3. Atmospherics due to thunderstorms, disturbance arising from charging and discharging processes under flight conditions, troubles caused by the formation of ice and hoarfrost on parts of the wireless equipment and damages done to the wireless set by atmospheric discharges such as lightning flashes are the main subjects dealt with.

22 pages with 15 figures.

D.5. **Fundamental and Practical Questions relating to Ionospheric Research**

Precis by Dr. Schwenkhagen of report in German No. D5 by ZENNECK

Method of taking soundings of the ionosphere by means of pulses with constant frequency or sliding frequency. Definition of virtual height of the different layers of the ionosphere. Discussion of partial reflexion of the electromagnetic waves in the lower layers. A considerable part of the paper is devoted to fundamental considerations of direction finding equipment and the influence of the ionosphere to the bearings. The paper concludes with a survey of the relations existing between the activity of the sun and ionospheric disturbances causing trouble to the propagation of waves.

24 pages with 20 figures.

A discussion on D2 to D5 is added to the report of the meeting.

D.6. **Radio Interference known as Hissing**

Precis by Dr. Schwenkhagen of report in German No. D6 by MEINHOLD

The special type of radio interference known as "hissing" is frequently called "precipitation static", because precipitation is often thought of to be the cause of such interference, though there are a lot of observations indicating hissing without any precipitations whatsoever. The author presents the results of simultaneous records of hissing and of the potential gradient of the atmospheric electric field. From these records evidence is taken that hissing is a mere electrostatic problem due to an interrupted (discontinuous but unidirectional) discharge of the antenna into the atmosphere as soon as a certain level of potential gradient is exceeded. This level depends upon the form of the antenna. Frequency and character of the hissing noice are bound to the excess of potential gradient over the critical value and its sign.

23 pages with 8 figures and 1 table.

D.7. **Recording of Atmospherics at 6 Mc per s.**

Precis by Dr. Schwenkhagen of report in German No. D7 by MEINHOLD

A device used for recording atmospherics in the 6Mcs/s-band is described. The records are discussed with regard to the number and amplitude of clicks. In order to arrive at a proper assessment of the interference with wireless reception due to the clicks an "interference level" is defined and derived from the records for a period of one year. Obviously the Interference Level depends upon meteorological conditions as well as upon the influence of cosmic phenomena to the wave propagation. Both of these factors are contributory to the quasiperiodical change of the Interference Level with time of day and its annual changes. The experimental results are in good agreement with the theory presented.

90 pages with 45 figures.

D.8. **Device for Recording the Level of "Clicks" (Atmospherics) and Results collected**

Precis by Dr. Schwenkhagen of report in German No. D8 by MEINHOLD

A modification of the device used for the research dealt with in a previous paper (D7) is described. Instead of a normal audio-frequency output meter used for the previous records a noise-level-meter is now preferred. Simultaneous records with both equipments form a connecting link between the previous results and the records for 1942 to 1944 presented in this paper. Diagrams of the interference level as an average for each month of the above period are given.

14 pages with 10 figures

D.9. **Locating of atmospherics as a Means of Weather-Forecasting**

Precis by Dr. Schwenkhagen of report in German No. D9 by SCHINDELHAUER, ISRAEL

2 equal loop-antennas arranged at right angles are connected to 2 equal superheterodyne receiving sets tuned to 27 kc per sec. The output connections are connected to the horizontal and vertical plates of a cathode ray oscillograph respectively, such as to move the spot of the tube in a direction corresponding to the direction of the atmospheric click. The screen of the tube is photographed with a high speed film-camera. Synchronous marks are given on the record tapes of 3 stations with a base of 650 miles by simultaneous recording of Morse-signals. The authors think the results obtained to be questionable for weather forecast.

40 pages with 45 figures.

D.10. **Report on the Meeting - Level of Atmospherics**

Precis by Dr. Schwenkhagen of report in German No. D.10 by SCHWENKHAGEN

Abridged reports of the papers presented and the following discussions at a meeting held in Danzig in April 1944.

A) Level of Atmospherics and its practical Importance (SCHWENKHAGEN)

Three types of atmospherics are classified: "Grinder" causing an almost continuous increase of output level of the receiver, Hissing known as a short-time high-level audio frequency output, and Clicks, i.e. abrupt pulses with a distinct time-clearance. Plenty of information is available about hissing and clicks, but only one series of informative tests have been carried out with respect to grinders. Atmospherics can be used for forecasting weather as well as ionospheric conditions. The impairing of wireless communications by hissing and clicks can be materially reduced by proper design of antennas and receivers. The level of grinders is the real limit to the useful sensitivity of receiving sets.   5 pages, 8 figures.

B) Nomenclature of Atmospherics (MEINHOLD)

A general standard nomenclature for atmospherics is suggested.
2 pages.

C) Extraterrestrial Interference to Wavelengths below 10 m (FRANZ).

Tests carried out by the author and his associates confirm the existence of an extraterrestrial source of electromagnetic waves in the range of 2 m to 16 m wavelength. The noise level due to it ranges from 40 to 400 kT for 10 m decreasing to about thermal noise level for 2 m. One definite point of the galactic system must be considered as the source.
4 pages, 3 figures.

D) Influence of more Elevated Layers of the Atmosphere upon Atmospherics (SCHINDELHAUER).

The author thinks that meteorological conditions cannot account for directional distribution of atmospherics found in previous research as well as in his own recent measurements. He, therefore, suggests the existence of some kind of radiation source in the ionosphere. His remarks are broadly discussed and mostly opposed by the rest of those present.
3 pages including discussion, 11 figures.

E) Discussion on the Necessity of a Broader Base for Fundamental Research.

Three main items are to be taken care of in the future:
1) Geographical distribution of the level of atmospherics,
2) Distribution of atmospherics with regard to wavelength,
3) Minimum atmospheric noise level as a limit for useful sensitivity.   2 pages.

F) Report on the Research Work regarding Atmospherics done by the Propagation Department of the Deutsche Reichspost. (BENDER)

The paper describes some recording devices that have been specially designed for recording atmospherics. They use electrolytic cells as indicating devices and counting type relays for the number of atmospheric clicks. Short Discussion.
2 pages, 2 figures.

G) Discussion with regard to Weather- and Ionosphere-Forecast by measuring the Level of Atmospherics.

Discussion to part of paper A (see above). A thorough investigation of weather forecasting is suggested.
2 pages.

H) Click Removing Set-ups (MEINHOLD)

The paper presents wiring diagrams for different kinds of click-elimination. Advantages and drawbacks of the different systems are discussed. The working conditions and results obtained are demonstrated for 5 different arrangements.

3 pages, 7 figures.

I) Click Elimination. (KAWAN)

According to a suggestion by the author, the signal in a receiver fitted with a click elimination arrangement by change of grid bias in the last intermediate frequency stage, should be delayed by means of a special network matched to the circuit of the suppressing tube. Design and results are broadly discussed. Short discussion.
6 pages, 1 figure.

D.11. **Records of Field Strength and Charging of Aircraft up to high Levels above the Ground**

Precis by Dr. Schwenkhagen of report in German No. D. 11 by
WITTICH, KASEMIR.

Flights up to a level of 3 to 5 miles brought evidence that the potential gradient of the atmospheric electric field rapidly decreases with the level above ground as soon as the dust layers of the lower atmosphere are left. The rest is of the order of 5 to 10 V/m. Normally the field is positive, negative fields occurring mostly under thunderstorm and similar conditions. Clouds carry space charge layers with opposite sign, positive charges being accumulated near the top layers. Field strength is much higher in clouds consisting of ice-crystals than in those made up by water-droplets. Space-charges in the dusty parts of the atmosphere range in density from 10^{-18} coulombs per cu.cm up to 10^{-16}. In thunderstorms they may be larger by 2 to 3 powers of 10.

22 pages with 11 figures.

D.12. **First Records of Atmospheric Field and Aircraft Charging with Generating Voltmeters in Gliding Planes**

Precis by Dr. Schwenkhagen of report in German No. D 12 by
LUEDER, KASEMIR, ROSZMANN.

The records of potential gradient and charge carried by a plane were obtained by using a generating voltmeter or rather a set of generating voltmeters installed in a highload-glider towed to a motor-plane during the ascent. The field rapidly decreases above the dusty layers near to the ground to 1o to 21 V/m. By the influence of the tugging motor-plane the glider charged up to a tension of about - 2ooo Volts: after declinching the glider charged up to - 30 ooo Volts when passing through precipitation of ice-crystals.

20 pages with 9 figures.

D.13. **First Records of Atmospheric Electric Conductivity up to High Levels above the Ground**

Precis by Dr. Schwenkhagen of report in German No. D 13 by
ROSZMANN

The tests reported were carried out in a highload-glider in order to avoid difficulties arising from the motor combustion gases of a normal plane. An electrometric device with one preamplifying stage was used for the measurement of the polar conductivities as well as of the number of ions of both signs separately. The equipment was of normal design using a highly insulated test-condenser charged by an auxiliary battery and discharged by the ions suspended in the air flow. There is no appreciable difference in both signs of the polar conductivity. The conductivity increases by about the factor 10 with increasing level up to 5 miles, such increase being normally bound to the upper limit of visible dust layers. Very large conductivities exceeding the normal values by about 2 powers of 10 were found to exist within strong vertical airflows due to thermal non mixing.

13 pages with 5 figures.

D.14 Device for Measuring the Atmospheric Electric Field Strength

Precis by Dr. Schwenkhagen of report in German No. D 14 by RANGS

A special design of a generating voltmeter is described. In addition to the normal electrostatic generator a magnetic induction type generator is mounted on the same axis. Its output voltage is connected in series with that of the electrostatic, but periodically shortcircuited. Thus the equipment automatically gives proof of any change of sensitivity due to changes in number of revolutions of the axis. The sign of the field strength is always known. Examples of records are given. Difficulties met with in the design are discussed. Practical applications are suggested.

53 pages with 32 figures and 1 table.

D.15 Measurements of Polar Electric Conductivity in the Free Atmosphere

Precis by Dr. Schwenkhagen of report in German No. D 15 by ROSZMANN

The evaluation of 85 flights presented in this paper confirm the conclusions drawn from former records reported by the same author in a previous paper (see D 13). Generally speaking the polar conductivity depends more upon local weather conditions than upon the general aspect of the meteorological state. A somewhat stronger correlation to the kind of air masses is suggested by the result of one test.

30 pages, 7 figures, 15 tables.

D.16.   Investigations of Charging Phenomena

Precis by Dr. Schwenkhagen of report in German No. D16 by VIEWEG

The papers deal with the possibilities of interference due to the impact of ice-crystals or water-droplets in the atmosphere on the aerial of a plane. According to his tests such interference probably occurs with charged as well as uncharged particles, the peak values being caused by charged ice-particles (sleet) at a temperature of about 32°F. Certain protective value is ascribed to semiconducting coating of the aerial, whereas insulating varnish coatings seem to be most disadvantageous.

12 pages with 13 figures.

D.17.   Electrostatic Charging of Planes
                 and a new Method of Prevention

Precis by Dr. Schwenkhagen of report in German No. D17 by DESSAUER.

Tests carried out by the author give evidence of the fact that static charging voltage and current of a plane depends in amplitude and sign upon the kind of fuel used for the engines. For each kind of fuel adding of traces of chemicals properly chosen reduces the charging effect to minute values, which easily can be disposed of by normal types of discharging equipment. The main additional substances used are CCl_4 and CH_2Br-CH_2Br. Both of them apparently have no corrosive effect on the fuel tanks.

13 pages and 17 figures.

D.18. New Type of Discharger for Removing Static Charges of Planes

Precis by Dr. Schwenkhagen of report in German No. D18 by MEINHOLD.

A new type of discharger using a hemp-tail with a Carbon coating is described. Laboratory tests of the device show high capacity for discharging current and low level of interference. The results obtained are equivalent in discharging quality to the tungsten point suggested by the DVL. Practical experience not yet available.

9 pages with 5 figures.

D.19.   Conductivity of Aircraft Spurwheel-Tyres and its Change under Service Conditions.

Precis by Dr. Schwenkhagen of report in German No. D 19 by BECKER

Tyres for aircraft are rendered conductive by adding soot to the rubber, in order to prevent the plane from becoming electrically charged when on the ground. The resistance measured under service conditions between the wheel-hub and the ground with 40 Volts d.c. applied should be well below 4 Megohms. This resistance always is increased by aging the tyres due to the mechanical stresses imposed on them especially by landing. For new tyres this resistance therefore should not exceed 40 kiloohms. The increase of resistance is mainly due to wear near the contact surface between metal and rubber. Changes of design to improve the properties are suggested.

16 pages with 7 figures and 2 tables.

D.20.   Most advantageous Design and Installation of Anti-Static Condensers up to 100 Mc per sec.

Precis by Dr. Schwenkhagen of report in German No. D.20 by GRADMAN, SCHMIDT.

The quotient of input-current to output-voltage is lowest for the bushing-type-condenser with the axis arranged in the direction of the connections. All other type of equipment shows considerable increase in this coupling impedance due to resonance of the condenser with the loop formed by the connections.

14 pages with 8 figures.

D.21.   Permissible Interference Voltage within the Main-Supply

Precis by Dr. Schwenkhagen of report in German No. D 21 by VIEHMANN, SCHMIDT.

Except for the shielding of the wiring between the interference generating parts of the main supply and the antistatic-devices installed for them and the shielding of antenna-leads all screening of the main supply may be disposed of without serious trouble to the receiving conditions in planes of the type Ju 88. Interference Voltages permitted by the Regulations of the Luftwaffe meet all practical requirements. For short-time interference generators an increase of permissible voltage by

5 timer normal value is suggested. Choking equipment should be inserted un the power supply of receivers (FUG 10) to prevent interference voltages from entering the receiver through the mains.

59 pages with 34 figures and 1 table.

F.1. **On hitherto unknown light-emitting phenomena in the middle layers of the ionosphere and their relation to wave-propagation.**

Precis by Dr. Schwenkhagen of report in German No. F.1. by
HOFFMEISTER

Luminous stripes visible to the naked eye are due to the impact of meteoric dust on the upper layers of the atmosphere according to the opinion of the authors. Disturbances of the ionospheric conditions at levels ranging from 50 to 100 miles obviously are strongly correlated to the phenomenon. Thanks to the annual return of the dust impact a forecast of the ionospheric disturbances is suggested.

F.2. **Cloud-level-metering with searchlight during daytime**

Precis by Dr. Schwenkhagen of report in German No. F2 by HANLE,
SCHMILLEN.
The beam of a 100% modulated searchlight is directed to the cloud. The illuminated spot on the cloud is located with a photo-electric set with an amplifier for a band-width of only 1 c. With the devices described, cloud levels up to 1 mile can be determined with sufficient accuracy by evaluating the triangle.

F.3. **Abnormal brightness of the sky during night-time**

Precis by Dr. Schwenkhagen of report in German No. F3 by HOFFMEISTER

Abnormal brightness of the nocturnal sky is apparently due to the same events as the luminous stripes (see F1). The color index varies according to brightness, the color moving towards the red end of the spectrum with increasing brightness. One may assume a considerable amount of infra-red radiation.

F.4.   **Thermo-elements for radiation measuring purposes**

   Precis by Dr. Schwenkhagen of report in German No. F4 by GEILING

   Contribution to the knowledge of Thermo-elements for radiation measuring purposes. (GEILING).
   Compilation of formula for the design of thermo-elements for radiation measurements. Definition of proper quality-indicating properties of the elements. Measurements and tables of physical properties of the materials used for practical design. Design of elements for "I.R.-retina".

F.5.   **Light scattered by the Atmosphere**

   Precis by Dr. Schwenkhagen of report in German No. F5 by SIEDENTOPF

   Report on tests carried out up to levels of 5.5 miles above ground with regard to light emission from the zenith and its spectral distribution.
   Derived herefrom are: Distribution of dust in the atmosphere, visibility of aircraft with various reflective power and limit of visibility of stars by daylight.

F.6.   Tests for Locating the Sun by means of Infra-red Radiation using Long-Range-Actinometer

L.1.   Vertical Beam Characteristics of Antennas Mounted on the Supporting Planes of Aircraft.

L.2. Selected information with regard to the Theory and Technology of Antennae.

(a) First Volume
1) General requirements raised by the army with regard to the properties and dimensions of fixed and portable aerials.
2) Transmitting aerials with narrow dimensions for floating structures and requirements of the navy for aerials aboard.
3) Beam-antennae with antenna-amplifiers.
4) Requirements of the air force with regard to beam antennae for long-distance range dm communication-channels.
5) Aircraft Antennae.
6) Exciting the planes of aircraft.
7) Aircraft aerials for short wave communications.
8) Long-line aerials mounted on the planes of aircraft.
9) Antenna and distance range.
10) Fundamental knowledge of beam antennae.
11) New type of short beam antenna with vertical polarization only.
12) Beam antenna system for dm and cm wavelength without feeders.
13) Ground-bound bearings antenna systems.
14) Direction finding loops with iron core.
15) Multiple use of transmitting antennae.
16) Anti-fading transmitting aerials.
17) Aerials for railway equipment.
18) Raw materials for aerials from viewpoint of the radio-engineer.
19) Regulations for standard denominations of antenna properties. to be used in papers and reports.

(b) Second Volume
1) Fundamental consideration of wideband-aerials.
2) Experimental research on sheet and tube dipoles as wideband aerials.
3) Influence of a reflecting wall to the impedance curve of tubular wideband dipoles.
4) Use of eel-buck and like antennae in the short-wave and ultra short waveband.
5) Compensation of dipole antennae near the footing-point.
6) Matching, testing and designing of a wideband dipole antenna.
7) Rotating wideband dipole (Codename Breitbein = Broadleg).
8) Installation of a huge wideband antenna.
9) On wideband antennae for long waves.
10) Dielectric cylinders as beam antennae for dm and cm waves.
11) Investigations of parabolic sheet antennae.
12) Calculation and design of wideband line transformers.
13) High frequency feeders and their matching.
14) Recent experience of the Deutsche Reichpost with antennae.
15) Damping of high frequency concentric feeding lines.
16) General considerations on wave guides.
17) Regulations for standard denominations of antenna properties.

L.3. Dipole Groups with high frequency Supply as End-Fire Arrays for wideband.

L.4. Contributions to the Arrangement of Dipole rows and Dipole-groups as end-fire arrays.

L.5. Wideband Yagi Antennae.

L.6. Coupling by Radiation between two dipoles fitted with reflectors First Part.

L.7. Coupling by Radiation between two dipoles fitted with reflectors Second Part.

L.8. Report of a Meeting concerning Beam Antennae aboard Aircraft.

1) Electromechanical Pattern for Ascertaining the Radiation Characteristic of Antenna-Groups.
2) Graphical computing of Radiation Characteristics of Antenna-Groups. Design of Beam Antennae. Properties of a new for of Antenna-Group.
3) Beam Antenna with extremely low by-peaks by Radiation.
4) Relations between Beam-Angle and amplitude of By-Peaks for fixed values of relative dimensions and number of Antennae.
5) Intersected Antenna with series-connected Condenser for Elimination of By-Peaks.
6) Investigations of Long-Wire-Antennae in dm Ranges.
7) Investigations regarding Aircraft-Red Antennae for the Ultra-Short-Wave-Range.
8) Investigations of Funnel-Antennae and Funnel-Groups.
9) Comparison of Funnel and Box Shaped Antennae.
10) A simple 5 m Beam Antenna for use aboard Aircraft.
11) Investigations of Aircraft Ultra-short-wave-Antennae for Vertical and Horizontal Shifting of the Beam.
12) Response of Receiving Aerials.

L.9. Radiation and Matching of Waveguides and Funnel shaped Antennae with dielectric Frontcover.

L.10. Properties of Funnel shaped Antennae in the Cm Range.

L.11. Investigations of Short Funnel shaped Beam Antennae.

L.12. Radiation Field inside a Rotary-Parabolic Mirror with an Axial Electric or Magnetic Dipole arranged in or in front of the Focus.

L.13. Large Technical Parabolic Mirrors. (2 parts A and B.)

M.1. **Measuring devices for magnetic fields with "Forster" pick-up**

Precis by Dr. Schwenkhagen of report in German No. M.1 by
                                                      FELBTKELLER

Theoretical considerations on the most advantageous dimensions of the highly permeable iron core for three types of Forster pick-up using 1) unbalance of audio-frequency Wheatstone Bridge for fundamental frequency, 2) phase shifting of induced pulse voltage, 3) unbalance of Wheatstone Bridge for first harmonic. Field strength measurement as well as measurement of difference in field strength are investigated.

M.2. **Deformation of the geomagnetic field by a hollow sphere.**

Precis by Dr. Schwenkhagen of report in German No. M.2. by TRAUB

Dipole field of a hollow permeable sphere in the geomagnetic field gives rise to a difference in magnetic field strength in two points arranged vertically above one another. The distribution of such difference along a horizontal line passing through the vertical axis of the sphere is calculated.

M.3. **Magnetic state of vehicles**

Precis by Dr. Schwenkhagen of report in German No. M.3 by LANGE

The magnetic properties of vehicles are due to the magnetic state of their parts arising from influences during construction as well as from the influence of the geomagnetic field during assembly. They are changed by vibrations in service. Checking the field of a model aircraft in homogeneous field with iron filings.

M.4. **Electromagnetic shields**

Precis by Dr. Schwenkhagen of report in German No. M.4 by SCHAFFER

Compilation of results given by previous literature with regard to shielding effect of screens for lines carrying audio- or high frequency currents. Theoretical and experimental results are considered.

M.5.   **Electromagnetic Sheilds**

Precis by Dr. Schwenkhagen of report in German No. M5 by
GRADMANN, SCHAFFER

Experimental investigations relating to the effect of small holes in electromagnetic screens for high frequency lines such as due to ventilating openings or broken strings in conducting wicker work.

N.1. The Ionosphere and its significance for the Wireless Communications of military Services.

N.2. Advices for the Proper Choice of Wavelength for military Communications given by the "Radio Advisory Office".

N.3. Handbook of Useful Short-wave Communications for 1943
    (2 copies a and b.)

N.4. Fundamental Diagrams of Wave Propagation for the whole Frequency Range (without influence of Ionosphere) (1st Edition)

N.5. Propagation of Earthbound Waves for the whole Frequency Range presented in the form of Graphs. (2nd Edition of N.4.)
    (5 copies a to e).

N.6. Tables for Calculating the Transmission Limiting Frequencies from Vertical Incidence limiting frequency due to reflexion at the Ionosphere.

N.7. E-Layer of the Ionosphere, daily and annual fluctuations.

N.8. The influence of damping to the propagation of Short-Waves.

N.9. Scattering of Frequency-Limits of the Ionosphere Layers.

N.10. "Index" method for the Forecast of ionospheric Frequency- Limits.

N.11. Propagation of electromagnetic Waves in a Medium arranged in Layers under the Influence of a Magnet Field for vertical Incidence.

N.12. On Disturbances of the ionospheric state due to Northern Lights and the Velocity of Propagation of such Disturbances.

N.13. The propagation of Electromagnetic Waves in a Medium arranged in Layers for various angles of Incidence.

N.14. Investigations of Polarization of Short-Wave Ionospheric-Echoes.

N.15. Propagation of Electromagnetic Waves in a Medium arranged in Layers under the Influence of a Magnetic Field for any angle of Incidence. 1st. Part.

N.16. Propagation of .... 2nd Part of N.15.

N.17. Contributions to the Structure of the Ionosphere.

N.18. Report on a Meeting of the "National Academy of Aircraft Research". (Deutsche Akademie fue Luftfahrtforschung).

1) On the limitations of accuracy for Direction Finding and Distance Metering With Radiowaves over large Distances.

2) The influence of the Atmosphere to the Propagation of Hyperfrequency-Waves.

3) Taking into Account the Activity of the Sun for Ionosphere Forecast.

N.19. On Investigation of molecular processes in the Ionosphere by means of the "Luxemburg-Effect".

N.20. On propagation phenomena of Fading of Ionospheric Echoes.

N.21. Deviation of Signals reflected by the Ionosphere from the direction of the Maximum Circle.

N.22. Indirect Signals and Signals around the Circumference of the Earth in the Short-Wave Range.

N.23. Long-Range Propagation of Short-Waves by means of Zigzag Reflexions: Reapplication to this Statement.

0.1.   **Modulation and Demodulation of FM Signals**

Precis by Dr. Schwenkhagen of report in German No. 0.1 by RUPP, NUSSLEIN, WEGENER.

A. pages 2 - 20 (Rupp). Methods of frequency modulation. Thoery and limiting factors for usual methods of FM. The paper deals with 1) Mechanical Wobbling, 2) Phase modulation of a quartz crystal stabilized low-frequency generator with final frequency-multiplying, 3) FM of high frequency circuits by connecting in parallel electronic tubes with reactive feedback.

B. pages 21-45 (Nusslein) Receiving methods for FM signals. In addition to normal receiving equipment FN receiving requires an amplitude limitation set and an inverter from FM to AM. The normal pentode-amplitude-limitor is discussed in full detail, followed by a theoretical investigation of the inverting power of networks the resistances of which depend upon the frequency applied. Removal of the carrier frequency according to the suggestions of Carson, Fry and Day are dealt with too. Finally, the effect of negative feedback for FM signals suggested by Chaffee is described.

C. pages 46-61 (Wagener) Signal transmitter for AM to FM. General requirements for AM and FM signal transmitters are presented. Wiring diagrams are given for a transmitter for 35 to 50 Mcs/s. The author gives details of the construction. The properties of the transmitter are tested and are indicated at the end of the paper.

0.2.   **Amplifier for 0.1 to 100,000 c/s for oscillographic purposes with 50 cycle supply**

Precis by Dr. Schwenkhagen of report in German No. 0.2 by KEUL

A special amplifier for 5 mV maximum input with 32 k ohm internal resistance was designed for use in connection with a cathode ray oscillograph (needed input 100 volts) or a loop-oscillograph (needed input 50 mA). Phase shift rises to $45°$ at 0.2 cycles and at 100 kilocycles. The r.m.s. value of all harmonics coming from the amplifier is less than 2% of the fundamental.

O.3. Deformation of pulses in amplifiers

Precis by Dr. Schwenkhagen of report in German No. O.3 by HUBER

For multi-stage amplifiers with a frequency curve of amplification and phase-shift given either by calculation or by testing the complete set, a simple numerical integration based on operational calculus allows for computing the wave shape of the output pulses for any form of input pulses. According to the fundamental investigations, it is found that for proper design the product of band-width of the amplifier and the length of the pulse should exceed 1. Symmetrical output pulses require a constant transit-time for all frequencies concerned. For high steepness of the pulse-front a considerable number of normal broad-band resonating circuits are preferred to the use of band-filters. Resonance amplifiers with a flat frequency response curve are disadvantageous on account of "creeping" in the front and oscillations in the rear of the pulse.

O.4. Design of Amplifiers for Pulse-Voltages in Connection with Time-measurements of high accuracy

Precis by Dr. Schwenkhagen of report in German No. O.4 by BREUNINGER

It is shown in this paper that in many cases it is advisable to make use of the pulse front instead of the peaks, because for this type of equipment the pulse-form is not of much importance. A theory for the design of amplifiers based upon this fundamental knowledge is presented. The paper especially deals with those cases where extremely high accuracy of timing (less than 10 s) is required.

87 pages, 3 tables, 17 figures

O.5. Precis by Dr. Schwenkhagen of report in German No. O.5 by FAULSTICH

Contents summarised under C 1.

62 pages, 19 figures.

0.6. **Contact-set for timing Pulses ranging from 10 to 150 ms.**

Precis by Dr. Schwenkhagen of report in German No. 0.6 by WILDE, LUETTICHAU

A polarized relay is operated by the discharge pulse of a condenser, which is previously charged to a voltage near to the break-down voltage of a three electrode glow-discharge tube. The time, during which the contact of the relay is closed, is started by a pulse applied to the grid of the tube; its end depends upon the time constant of the discharge circuit varied by means of a resistance. Scheme of connections and results are given.

9 pages, 7 figures.

0.7. **Phase-Shifting and Measuring Devices**

Precis by Dr. Schwenkhagen of report in German No. 0.7 by MOELLE

It is suggested that use be made of a goniometric device for shewing variable phase of a constant voltage of definite frequency. This voltage is taken from a moving coil arranged in the rotating field of two crossed coils supplied with currents dephased by 90. The phase measuring device described in the second part of the paper is to be independent of the difference in amplitude of the two voltages to be compared. This is afforded by connecting two voltages tapped across equal resistances, which are connected in series with oppositely reactive elements, in series and in counter-series comparing their relative amplitude with 2 equal - or by means of additional resistances equalized - detecting elements in a d.c. milliameter.

21 pages, 24 figures.

Q.1. Report of a Meeting for High Frequency Measurements.

1) Detector-Measurements carried out at the PTR.
2) Absolute Determination of Frequency and Wavelength.
3) Wavemeters for the dm and cm ranges.
4) Cavity-Resonator Wavemeter for 9 to 12 cm Wavelength with absolute accuracy of 10⁻
5) Thermal Voltmeter for use up to 10 cm without Tuning.
6) Impedance Bridges in the m and dm Ranges as Complementary Equipment to Measuring Lines.
7) Power and Current Standards in the High Frequency Field.
8) Current Metering and Power Metering.
9) Measurements of Dielectric Constant and Losses of Insulating Materials at cm Waves.
10) Measurements of Damping in the dm and cm Ranges with Cathode Ray Indicator Tubes.
11) Measuring Wave-Guide for Wavelengths of 5 to 5o cm.
12) Development of a Measuring Line requiring a low amount of Material and Working time.
13) Metering the Properties of Quadrupoles with Measuring Lines.
14) Demonstration of dm-Metering Equipment. Circle shaped Measuring Line with Optical Display of the Distribution of Voltage along the Line (2 copies a and b.)

Q.2. Short Wave Metering Device Suggested by Malsch.

Q.3. Pick-up Devices for High Frequency Radiating Bodies.

Backheating in Magnetrons.

Precis by Dr. Schwenkhagen of report in German No. R 1 by DOHLER.

Investigation of backheating in a nonslotted magnetron in nonoscillating state by measurements of the grid current: it is found out, that Gas-ions cannot be the cause of backheating. It can be removed by applying a positive bias to a grid. The author presumes backheating to be due to the impact on the cathode of electrons, which have been accelerated by stray-effects when passing other electrons.

16 pages, 8 figures.

Oscillating Ranges for Short-Wave-Frequencies in Nonslotted Magnetrons.

Precis by Dr. Schwenkhagen of report in German No. R 2 by RAKELMANN.

Theoretical and experimental survey of short-wave oscillations occurring in nonslotted magnetrons. 4 different ranges of oscillations are clearly found. The oscillating mechanism for three of them is deduced.

25 pages, 21 figures.

Theory and Practical Experience with Transit-Time-Tubes.

Precis by Dr. Schwenkhagen of report in German No. R 3 by RATHEISER, SCHIFFEL.

Physical account of the happenings in magnetrons based upon fundamental considerations in Part I. The magnetic field in the magnetrons acts in the same way as the positive grid bias in a triode generating Barkhausen-Oscillations, the electrons moving on cycloid-formed paths around the cathode instead of swinging in rectilinear paths. The much more complicated oscillating process is studied and dealt with in detail. The different kinds and forms of oscillation (Transit-time oscillations and oscillations not bound to transit-time, roll-circle and path-oscillations) in connection with number of slots and order of oscillating range are discussed.

Finally the characteristics of the tubes are shown. Advice is given how to use the curves.

92 pages with 71 figures.

Properties of Magnetrons. Part III: Tubes of RD 2 Mh-Type.

Precis by Dr. Schwenkhagen of report in German No. R 4 by REICHEL, WANDER.

The tube RD 2 Mh is a magnetron with 8 slots and capacitive-coupled load. The cathode is indirectly heated and has a Barium-oxide coating. It is designed to generate wavelengths in the 6 cm range with a magnetic field of 1500 Gauss. Experiments have shown that the wavelengths can be changed from 5.5 to 7.5 cm with a fixed normal field of 1500 Gauss. A certain extension of this range towards longer waves can be realised by decreasing the magnetic field strength at a sacrifice in output.

4 pages, 5 figures.

Generation of Cathode Rays with high Current Density.

Precis by Dr. Schwenkhagen of report in German No. R 5 by HECHTEL.

It is stated that there is a need for cathode ray beams of high current density with electrons moving along parallel paths for use in Klystrons and similar tubes. The author presents a theoretical and experimental investigation of the methods of establishing such beams. With accelerating voltages up to 2000 volts he succeeds in establishing beams of 0.3 sq. cm. cross section and some cm length, the current density being as high as about 8 to 9 Amps per square-inch. For stretching out the paths of the electrons to parallel lines a homogenous magnetic field is used in addition to electrical lenses.

33 pages with 24 figures.

Contributions to the Theory of Speed-controlled Transit-Time-Tubes with nonnegligible dimensions of the controlling and loading fields

Precis by Dr. Schwenkhagen of report in German No. R 6 by HOLLMANN, MASING, THOMA.

For hyperfrequency (e.g. cm wavelengths) the transit-time of the electrons between the two grids of the speed-modulating space (controlling field) is long enough to account for an appreciable phase angle between entering and leaving current. This paper deals with the effects of such phase angles, showing that there are harmonics due to this fact and that the degree of modulation in density of the fundamental frequency decreases. The compression-bunches of electrons due to such non-linear behaviour of the tube and the delivery of output-energy to a quasistatic load field are calculated. In the second part the transit-time effects in the load-field are taken care of. It is regarded as an ultradynamic double-layer passed by a disinterrupted electronstream. It is shown that it is sufficient for practical purposes to take note of the energy of the fundamental frequency only.

67 pages with 19 figures.

The Klystron with Nonnegligible Transit-Time

Precis by Dr. Schwenkhagen of report in German No. R 7 by DAHLKE, LABUS.

For the generation of very short electromagnetic waves matching the resonating system to the Klystron i.e. to its electronic beam supplying the high-frequency energy is of utmost importance. This problem is thoroughly investigated upon the basis of the equations of movement of electrons. It is shown that finite transit-time-phase-angles in the controlling as well as in the loading fields are to be preferred. Phase angles of 180 degrees are especially advantageous. In this case the maximum efficiency attainable would be about 26%.

38 pages with 6 figures.

Contributions to the Theory of Speed-controlled Transit-Time-Tubes with increase E.H.T.

Precis by Dr. Schwenkhagen of report in German No. R 8 by MASING.

After a short introduction on the use of electron-time-tables an additional approximation theory for the calculation of density modulation by WEBSTER'S methods is suggested. For high voltages graphical methods are developed. Reference to practical design is made.

49 pages with 19 figures.

The Klystron with Nonnegligible Transit-Time and finite Modulation in the Controlling and Loading Spaces.

Precis by Dr. Schwenkhagen of report in German No. R 9 by HECHTEL.

No exact calculation of the happenings in a Klystron seems to be possible. The approximations used up to now are disproved by practical experience. The author therefore uses a combination of numerical and graphical solution to approach the problem, which cannot deal with all variables concerned. His calculations only refer to the case of a symmetrical twin-cavity-Klystron with equal length and equal amplitude and phase of the high frequency field in both the controlling and the loading field. Maximum efficiency of 36% is bound to the use of transit-time phase angles of 0.8 and 2.6.

15 pages with 5 figures.

S.1. Influence of Inhomogeneous Properties of the Ground to the Electromagnetic Field near to the Ground.

S.2. Pre-Testing of Direction Finding Fields with a Conductivity-Meter (Dipole Metering Method)

S.3. Influence of Inhomogeneous Properties of the Ground to Station Bound Errors of the Bearings.

S.4. Tests to take unobjectionable Bearings during the nightime in the Neighbourhood of Reflectors (2 copies a and b).

S.5. Location of Radio Soundings by means 25 cm Waves beamed with Mirrors.

S.6. Deviation from Maximum Circle and Refraction Phenomena in the Ionosphere.

Contribution to the Theory of Sidebands and of "Sway-Vector" Representation of Frequency-Modulation.

Precis by Dr. Schwenkhagen of report in German No. T 1 by ZINKE, STABLEIN.

A) pages 1 to 28. (ZINKE) Sidebands and Sway-vector Representation of F M Signals with sinusoidal and rectangular modulation.

The author aims at presenting a simple theory of FM by representing the FM signal in a vectordiagram with swaying vectors (pointers). Such diagrams allow for a simple estimate of the spectrum of the modulated high frequency signal, for small as well as for large depth of modulation. It applies to sinusoidal as well as to rectangular modulation. The conditions are especially clear for the case of rectangular modulation in telegraphy.

B) pages 29 to 72. (STABLEIN) Some consequences derived from the theory of sidebands and of sway-vector representation of frequency modulated signals.

It is shown that AM systems may be considered as linear networks to a certain extent. FM systems, however, are always of the nonlinear type, giving rise to additional sideband frequencies as soon as there is more than one modulation-frequency. In spite of these difficulties the rules of FM can easily be established when using the sideband theory of modulation for a sway-vector representation of the signal. In the main part the disturbing influence of interference-frequencies to the frequency-spectrum and the influence of reactive circuits is discussed.

2 Parts. 72 pages in the first volume.
13 + 38 figures in the second volume.

A Mechanical Balance-like System for Harmonic Analysis and Synthesis.

Precis by Dr. Schwenkhagen of report in German No. T 2 by WALZ.

Description of a harmonic analiser which may also be used for a harmonic synthesis. The equidistant values of the function to be analised are represented by the length of levers with a fixed load. The levers are coupled to a common axis by means of a pattern for each harmonic coefficient to be determined. The resulting mechanical moment of the axis is proportional to the coefficient. On account of the high accuracy of mechanical balances the internal errors should be smaller than those coming from outside the instrument.

14 pages, 8 figures.

Device for automatic control of given functional curves.

Precis by Dr. Schwenkhagen of report in German No. T 3 by DREYER.

For mathematical instruments two-way movable pointers are often used, which must be set by hand to follow a given curve. In order to avoid the introduction of errors into the result on account of the personal element a device has been designed for an automatic control of such pointers by means of photo-electric cells. The accuracy of the setting is to be about 0.1 mm.

15 pages, 12 figures.

The Elimination Method of GAUSS for the solution of Linear Equation Systems.

Precis by Dr. Schwenkhagen of report in German No. T 4 by ZURMUHL.

The elimination method of GAUSS for the solution of linear systems of equations is described in an elementary way. Important advices are given with regard to the advantageous procedure and arrangement of the evaluation for practical purposes. The question of proofs, attainable accuracy and the possibilities of further approach to the exact solution are discussed.

23 pages, 3 tables.

Solution of systems of linear equations by means of card index machines.

Precis by Dr. Schwenkhagen of report in German No. T 5 by DREYER.

The Gauss eliminating system for the solution of linear systems of equations in the modification of JORDAN offers a chance for the use of card index calculating machines of the so-called Hollerith-System. After short instruction personnel not trained in mathematics can be used for this task. In the paper the solution of 20 equations for 20 x's is given as an example. Normal index cards allow for the coefficients to be given to 7 figures. By making use of repeated proofs the results can be given to an accuracy of 7 figures too. The solution was arrived at within 65 hours. This time can be shortened to about 40 to 45 hours when introducing certain simplifications. Each step for increasing the accuracy of the result takes only 5 hours.

19 pages, 8 tables.

Recent Simple electrical Calculating Machines for Automatic Solving of complicated Calculating Operations.

Precis by Dr. Schwenkhagen of report in German No. T 6 by HOPPE.

By means of sliding tap resistances or the like a mechanical mathematical function is changed into a corresponding electric voltage. Connecting such voltages in series allows for representation of mathematical series in the resulting voltage. Square formed resistance discs with two taps connected to the centre and sliding round a circle allow application of a sinusoidal voltage. Coupling the axis of such discs with toothed wheels gives the result of a Fourier-series. A model is described. Results of the automatical calculation are compared to the results of traditional calculations and found to be satisfactory.

32 pages with 9 figures and 1 table. Appendix 3 pages.

Testing of Materials for Resistance Potentiometers.

Precis by Dr. Schwenkhagen of report in German No. U 1 by LINCKH, RUMP.

Investigations have been made to reduce wear in potentiometer elements. Tests carried out by the author show that these difficulties can materially be reduced by the use of silver-rolls as sliding taps and submerging the equipment in oil. Instead of an alloy of silver and palladium less expensive raw materials such as constantan or chrome-nickel alloys can be used for the winding.

11 pages with 14 figures.

Testing of Contact Materials.

Precis by Dr. Schwenkhagen of report in German No. U 2 by LINCKH, RUMP.

A specially designed vibrating contactor tuned to resonance for 100 c/s is used in testing materials for contacts at a tension below the minimum arcing voltage with two values of current. The migration of material is determined for both electrodes for millions of switching operations. A large number of photographs on an enlarged scale show the form of deformation of the surface. All experiments are compiled for a table which facilitates the proper choice of material for practical switching equipment.

39 pages with 51 figures.

Testing of Contact Materials.

Precis by Dr. Schwenkhagen of report in German No U3 by LINCKH, RUMP.

Measurements of the change of contact resistance for 36 contact materials after a prolonged period of storage under tropical weather conditions (42 degrees Celsius and relative humidity 70%) are carried out for different pressures applied to the contact. The results are plotted in diagrams arranged in a qualitative order of approval.

46 pages with 37 figures.

Testing of Contact Materials.

Precis by Dr. Schwenkhagen of report in German No. U 4 by LINCKH, RUMP.

Contact-alloys of gold and silver as substitutes for Platinum and silver-palladium alloys of gold or silver with other metals are taken into consideration. The properties of these materials, i.e. perseverance of contact resistance, migration of materials and liability for welding of contact surface are checked. For some of these materials the results are good enough for practical use.

63 pages with 29 figures and 3 tables.

Testing and preparing of Contact Materials.

Precis by Dr. Schwenkhagen of report in German No. U 5 by SCHENCK, NICKELL.

On account of the shortage of platinum in Germany, alloys of more common metals such as gold were considered as substitutes. A number of gold-alloys has been tested with regard to the mode of preparation, possibilities of treatment, anti-corrosive properties in various atmospheric conditions and migration under d.c. switching conditions below the arcing level. Alloys of 95% gold with 5% Ga and of 80% gold with 10% Pt and 10% Ni proved to be the best ones. Alloys of molybdenum instead of gold should even be superior.

15 pages with 21 figures and 3 tables.

Testing of Contacts made out of noble Materials or Alloys of Noble Metals.

Precis by Dr. Schwenkhagen of report in German No. U 6 by ROSZ, UMMINGER, BRANDMULLER, HEUMANN.

According to the theory of HOLM the contact-resistance consists of two parts, the narrow pass resistance only depending upon the electric conductivity of the material, the pressure applied to the contact and its elastic or plastic properties on one hand, and a surface layer or skin resistance due to the existence of a mostly monomolecular layer of atoms other than the contact materials. The resistance of this layer ranges to about 5×10^{-9} Ohm.cm^2. Changes of the resistance with ageing of the contact is a natural consequence of elastic properties. Experiments show that the theory of HOLM holds well for all results. Thin layers of oil between the contact surface scarcely increase the resistance, but efficiently protect the surface against chemical influences.

62 pages with 35 figures and 6 tables.

On the Distance Range of Ultraviolet Radiation in the Atmosphere near the Ground.

Precis by Dr. Schwenkhagen of report in German No. U 7 by KOCH.

For wavelengths ranging from ultraviolet of 250 /u up to the near infrared of 1000 /u including the range of visible light the transparency of the atmosphere under different sight conditions is measured. Photoelectric equipment is used for the tests. Simultaneous tests of the noise level in the same band indicate that a distance range of 10 km is possible for the transmission of signals with wavelengths exceeding 310 /u. Though the noise level is extremely low for shorter wavelengths the distance range for these waves is limited to about 2 km due to the lack of proper transmitting and receiving equipment.

67 pages with 20 figures.

Ice-Coating of aerials and Preventing Measures.

Precis by Dr. Schwenkhagen of report in German No. U 8 by EDER.

Tests carried out with regard to the dielectric constant and the dielectric losses of ice give the necessary information for evaluating the influence of an ice-coating of plane-aerials and their insulating supports. The calculations refer to the power losses, the change of reactive resistance of the antenna connected to a corresponding detuning of the antenna circuit and to the overall efficiency of the transmitter antenna. As preventive measures heating with high-frequency, resistance heating with d.c. or a.c., proper antenna profiles are taken into consideration. Heating the antenna and its supports with resistances is declared the best form and is proved by flying tests.

51 pages with 30 figures and 1 table.

V.1. Lines used as Transformers and Measuring Elements.

V.2. Elimination of reflection due to joints and supports of Concentric Lines.

V.3. A new method for Broad-Band Matching especially for the dm and cm Range.

V.4. Broad Band Matching of various Half wavelength Dipoles by means of two homogeneous Linesections.

V.5. Which values are best characterising the Properties of Filtering Equipment in the dm and cm. Ranges.

W.1. Investigations of Waveguides.

W.2. Which values are best Characterising the Properties of Filtering Equipment in the dm and cm Ranges. (See V.5.)

W.3. Comparison of Arrangements during normal symmetrical lines and Waveguides with regard to the Dependency upon Frequency.

W.4. On the influence of Diaphragms in Rectangular Waveguides.

W.5. On Joints of Coaxial Lines in Waveguides.

W.6. Definition of Wave-Resistance and Measuring Technics.

W.7. The most simple types of TM and TE Waves in Waveguides.

W.8. Propagation Velocity, Wave Resistance and Damping of Electromagnetic Waves along Dielectric Cylinders.

W.9. Self-Contained Nonquasistationary Resonant Circuits.

W.10. Concentric Spheres as Electromagnetic Cavity Resonator.

W.11. Cofocal Ellipsoid shaped shells as Electromagnetic Cavity Resonator.

W.12. Magnetical Fundamental Frequency of Ellipsoid-shaped Cavity Resonators.

W.13. On the Excitation of Cavity Resonators.

W.14. Excitation of Circular Cavity Resonators by means of Density modulated Beams of Slow Electrons. Part 1. (4 copies a to d.)

W.15. Excitation of .... Part 11 of W.14. (4 copies a to d).

W.16. Contributions to the problem of Stability and Stabilization of Frequency of self excited Transmitters in the dm and cm Ranges.

W.17. Generator of Harmonics for Frequency Metering Purposes.

W.18. On Receiving Methods for cm-Waves.

W.19. On a Rectifying Device suggested by Doehler.

X.1. Propagation of Ultra-Short Waves.
1) Hitherto Existing Knowledge of Propagation Conditions and the possibilities of Practical Use of Ultra Short Waves.
2) On propagation Conditions and possibilities of using Ultra Short Waves with special regard to Aircraft Communications.

X.2. Quartz-Controlled Oscillators for the Ultra-short-Wave Range.

    I Part; Investigations of Quartz Crystals for the Control of Ultra Short Waves.

    II Part; Investigations of Quartz Controlled Oscillating Arrangements for variable Frequency in Ultra-Short Wave Range.

X.3. Interference Phenomens for vertical Incidence of Waves to the Ground.

Y.1. Indicating Device for Radar Equipment.

Y.2. Fundamental Rules for the Design of Pulse Transformers.

Y.3. Taking into account the effect of Polarization for Bending and Relection of Electromagnetic Waves.

Y.4. Influence of the Pulse-Shape of reflected signals to the Distance Range and Accuracy of Distance Metering.

Y.5. Results of Short Wave Pulse Transmission Tests.

Y.6. Continuous Wave Reflected Signal Method for Indicating the Presence of Aircraft (Codename Luchs-Danzig)

Y.7. On the relations between Characteristic and response of Detectors used in the Rotterdam Equipment.

Y.8. Investigation of the Rotterdam Pulse Generating Set.

Y.9. Wiring Diagrams and Photos of Parts, Accessories and of Screen Pictures of the Meddo Equipment.

Y.10. American Hyperfrequency Television Equipment Meddo.

Z.1. National Report of Physics (Restricted) Number 1.

1) Ultra violet absorption spectrum of the Suphides and Oxydes of zinc and Cadmium.
2) Structure and State of thin layers of Germanium
3) Bending of Electrons by Alloys of copper and zinc
4) Silica-glass as a sturdy, temperature-proof and acidproof Supportfoil for electronic interference and electronic microscopes.
5) On Back scattering of slowly moving Neutrons by matter containing Hydrogene.
6) Tests carried out regarding Ultra violet counters.
7) Increasing the response of Thermal Receiving Equipment for Low Temperature Radiation.
8) Decline of Brightness and Change of Colour during Dawn.
9) On spectroscopic proof of minute traces of water.
10) Attempts for the increase of Output of 18n Beam tubes by means of Condenser Discharges.
11) Electrostrictive Generation of Ultrasonic Frequencies.

Z.2. National Reports of Physics (Restricted) Number 2.

1) The Anode Flame of High Current Carbon-Arc.
2) On the establishing of Ion Beams.
3) Conditions of Resonance and Dee-Form for Cyclotrons.
4) Directional Distribution of Light Absorption of graphite.
5)

Z.3. National Reports of Physics (Restricted) Number 3.

1) Field properties and Beam Establishing in Cathode Ray Tubes
2) Contributions to the Working Conditions of Heterodyne-Stages for dm and cm. Receiving Sets.
3) Fine Migration of Matter from Opening Contacts.
4) Emission of secondary Electrons from crystallic Phosphorescent Matter with high speed primary Electrons.

Z.4. National Reports of Physics (Restricted) Number 4 (2 copies)

1) Accelerated Polymerization by the impact of Roentgen Radiation.

Z.4. (Contd.)

2) Suitability of ballistic Pendulums for generating and metering of short contact times.
3) The Cathode Flame of High Current Carbon Arc.
4) On a Method of Fixing the Number of Pulses in Counter Tubes for frequent Pulses.
5) On internal molecular Sensiblization of Phosphorescent Matter.

Z.5. Signs of Voltages and Currents in Vacuum Tube Circuits. Translation of a Paper published in Communications.

REPORT I

TECHNICAL REPORT ON ERNST LECHER INSTITUTE

An Institute under the Reichstelle fur Hochfrequenzforschung.

1. **TARGET NO:** Opportunity; first reported by EEIS

2. **TITLE OF TARGET:** Ernst Lecher Institute

3. **LOCATION:** Evacuated from Reichenau, near Wiener Neustadt to Seespitz Hotel, Plansee, near Reutte, (D295805). A portion of the institute is in a mill at Reutte (D345845).

4. **INVESTIGATING TEAM;** comprised some to the workers of CIOS trips No. 182 & 197
    Lt.Col. (acting) R.G. Friend   Ministry of Supply
    Major W.H. Maddison   "   "   "
    S/Ldr (acting) S. Devons   M.A.P.
    Mr. R.A. Soderman   A.B.L.15

5. **CONTENTS OF REPORT:**

    Section A. Report on preliminary discussion with Dr. Plendl and Dr. Hutter.

    " B. Report on the technical work in progress and completed.

    " C. List of personnel at the Seespitz and Reutte laboratories with place of birth, age, and subject in which they have been or are specialising.

    " D. List of reports, both final and internal prepared by the Institute.

    " E. List of such reports removed.

    " F. List of reports held by Dr. Plendl (comprising reports issued by the institute).

    " G. List of reports under F removed.

    " H. Financial position of the Institute, action taken etc.

SECTION A

Interrogation of Dr. Plendl of the Ernst Lecher Institut, at Plansee, near Reutte, 16/17 May 1945.

1. The interrogation of Dr. Plendl, the director of the Ernst Lecher Institut, was made by Lt. Col. Friend, Major Maddison, Sq. Ldr. Devons and Mr. Soderman. Throughout the interview Dr. Huter, a member of Dr. Plendl's staff, assisted with interpretation. He spoke English well having studied in the U.S.A. and lived in England. Every assistance was given by Dr. Plendl and his staff in our investigation and they behaved in the frankest possible manner. They expressed a desire to continue research either on their present problems or in accordance with such other directives as they might be given. Their attitude to the war seemed a dispassionate one and their principle interest science for its own sake. Certainly there is a considerable ability in the staff of the organisation.

2. **History of the Ernst Lecher Institut**

2.1 Dr. Plendl had directed the work of a group before the war upon the problems of the ionosphere and navigation. This work was sponsored by Telefunken and Luft-Hansa and was alleged to have been directed to civil aviation applications. The work was concerned largely with rotating beacons and the formation of navigational "grids" by the intersection of multi-lobed beacons. This work was on 1 to 6 metres wavelength. Work upon navigation by pulse methods was also started but did not reach fruition. It was mentioned that in 1934, at the suggestion of Drs. Kunholt (of N.V.K.) and Ruger, Plendl had investigated the reflection of radio beams from aircraft.

2.2 In 1938 the efforts of Dr. Plendl's group was directed to the military problems of navigation, blind bombing and radio altimeters. During this period and the earlier years of the war little fundamental work was done, the main occupation being the improvement of existing equipments.

2.3 Early in the war, various scientists had advocated the development of centimetric radar but the official policy adhered rigidly to the longer waves of the previously developed equipments. Although monitoring and aerial photography had disclosed that centimetric radars were being used in southern England it was not till the finding of an H2S (known as Rotterdam from the place of its capture) late in 1943 that any interest was shown in centimetric radars. No basic research had been done on H.F. technique since 1941, when all projects which could not then be completed in a year were stopped. In something of a panic the B.H.F. was formed to make up arrears by co-ordinating the work of existing institutes, the formation of new ones and the direction of industrial research on associated problems. Dr. Plendl handed over his existing work on navigational methods to Dr. Kunholdt of Kothen, where development and research for the improvement of existing systems was done, and undertook the direction of B.H.F. Among his first activities he founded about fifteen institutes for basic research, one of which was the Ernst Institut. Apparently the urge was to copy the captured British sets and Plendl's expensive programme of basic work was viewed unfavourably. Accordingly Dr. Esau took over the direction of B.H.F. and Plendl took over the direction of the Ernst Lecher Institut founded for investigation of centimetric technique. The laboratories of the latter were set up at Sessering Resortplatz, Reichenau near Wiener Neustadt with a total staff of about 200. When the Russian advance threatened, the Institute evacuated about 80 of its staff (including 20 qualified scientists and engineers) to its present location at Plansee near Reutte. About 70% of the better equipment was brought and a further 20 tons reached Hopfgarten near Kitzbuhel in three railway trucks where it rests at present. In addition to the main laboratory set up in the Seespitz Hotel at Plansee, a high vacuum laboratory was set up in Reutte. The latter place had been damaged and looted by occupying troops but was being put into operation again. Within the restrictions imposed by Military Government upon radio operation the laboratory was continuing its investigations.

3. Survey of investigations

3.1 The main task allotted initially was the development of centimetric aerials. They were fully informed of the details of the captured British equipment and the intended applications. Work started on centimetric Yagis, formed by inserting metal rods in a dielectric guide but little success was achieved and work was then directed to slotted waveguides. Apparently the relative smallness of German Aircraft caused some worry about fitting in the aerials of airborne equipment and with a singular failure to appreciate the significance of aerial aperture this work on Yagis and dielectric aerials had been in the hope of producing something smaller than a parabolic reflector. The mistake was now realised. The work on slotted waveguides was with the intention of producing an aerial which could be fitted into the leading edge of a wing, but at present was still advanced no further than the properties of a single slot and much had yet to be learned about the properties of guides in general. No work was being done on broad band aerials and reference was made to Prof. Sinker of the Fassbender Institut and also the Lorenz Company on this. Studies of the effect of inaccuracy in the parabolic reflector and production of beam split from a paraboloid were in hand. It seemed evident that they are in an elementary stage of centimetric technique.

3.2 A study had been made of the optimum parameters for good resolution on a German version of H2X (Meddo). For this purpose artificially generated echos were used. They were aware of the allied use of a super-sonic trainer and although one had been proposed to test "Berlin" they were not using this method for their tests.

3.3 Some work had been done upon artificial targets of the corner reflector type and also balloons coated with a mixture of oil and graphite. The latter seem to have been successful. It was mentioned that corner reflectors on floats had been used as camouflage of the Potsdam lakes against H2S and H2X observation. Although their tests had shown that the former was successful the reflectors had not proved sufficiently accurate for the shorter wavelengths.

3.4 Pulses as short as 1/10th microsec. had been produced for testing receivers but as Telefunken said that magnetrons take 1/3 of a microsec. to start oscillating no application had been made to transmitters of pulses shorter than one microsec. Apparently the word of Telefunken was accepted on such a matter and independent checks were not made. It was explained that there was always a drive upon them to produce something and many points which they would like to investigate had to be omitted.

3.5 Some work was being done upon local oscillators, where again Telefunken had decreed that magnetrons would be used. They were not investigating klystrons. No valve work had been done but part of the purpose in setting up a high vacuum laboratory had been for such work.

3.6 Crystals were developed by a Prof. Ott of Wurzburg but the Institute had made a number of tests on them. They were still far from satisfactory. The usual material used was synthetic pyrites with a tungsten loop contact, but germanium and tellurium were also used. The impression gained was that manufacturing and testing technique is inferior to our own and so are the results. Attempts had been made to use diode mixers but the return to crystals had been rapid. No attempts had been made by the institute to develop R.F. amplifiers for centimetric use but they were aware that attempts had been made both by F.F.O. and Telefunken.

3.7 Studies had been made of feeder and T-R section design.

3.8 Apparently it had not been found possible to reproduce the saturated tetrode used in the American A.P.S. 15 modulator and attempts were being made to replace it by a saturated diode.

3.9 Having started late in the centimetric field Dr. Plendl was now pushing down into the millimetre region. Work was in progress on 3, 1.5, and 0.8 cm. waves while it was mentioned that other investigators in the infra red region had gone up to .5 mm. The Czerny technique for the detection of infra-red was being adapted for the detection of millimetre waves in the laboratory in Reutte. It was hoped to develop a means by which an image of an object irradiated with millimeter waves could be focussed by a ceramic lens on to a Czerny diaphragm carrying a matrix of tiny dipoles and so produce an image which was rendered visible by the interference patterns created by the evaporation of a thin layer of oil around the excited dipoles. At this stage the principles were being established using 8mm radiation and wax lenses. Much shorter waves would be required to avoid the effects on interference in the "optical" system.

3.10 Jamming had thoroughly upset German Radar and in common with most other establishments the Ernst Lecher Institut was trying to make its contribution to the subject. Apparently after the Hamburg raid in 1943 when window was used a steadily increasing effort had been directed to A.J. methods. Within a month 20 Wurzburgs were equipped with "Wurzlaus" developed by Fach of the Muller Institut in Hamburg. Since then most Wurzburgs had been equipped with this or an improved system. All the methods used have utilised the Doppler effect to distinguish the aircraft which is moving from the stationary window. Following the Wurzlaus was a system, Tastlaus, developed by a Dr. Pohlman of R.L.M. which was easier to adjust and permitted a readier change of frequency. Then came Windlaus which permitted correction for drift velocity of the window. The contributions of the Ernst Lecher Institut were the Schiebelaus and the Reisslauss both of which were methods of correcting for wind drift by phase shifting the output of the coherent oscillator. The first actually moves the phase by a motor driven goniometer while the second momentarily changes the frequency of the COHO by a voltage pulse. These are still in the laboratory. A modification of the Reisslaus for application to Freyas is called Freyalaus and uses a reactance valve to change frequency.

3.11 Other devices mentioned, though not developed here were Taurus which improves target discrimination by differentiation of the video, and Nurnburg which aids following of targets at crossing point, when the Doppler Frequency is zero, by audible presentation of the propellor modulation. It was admitted that the recurrence frequency and split made the task difficult but filters were inserted and it was alleged that it was an aid to a skillful operator. Incidentally it was mentioned that girls were used as radar operators and had proved to be efficient. Also ground clutter was reduced by the erection of wire screens around Wurzburgs up to dipole height.

3.12 Distribution of frequencies had been a method of countering jamming and in the case of Freyas Yagi aerials had been produced, it was stated, up to 10 metres wavelength. This latter work had been done at Kothen and explains some of the Freya aerials found there though they were not of such a wavelength as that stated.

3.13 An interesting development at this institute is another A.J. device intended for Wurzburg application. This scheme uses a delay line to produce pulse cancellation and additional refinements are claimed to eliminate C.W. jamming and to improve the signal noise ratio apparently by pre-detector integration.

3.14 It was interesting to note the limited knowledge possessed by the Ernst Lecher Institut of Allied ground radar. Although it was known that British GL equipment had been captured in France 1940 and later in N.Africa they seemed to have no knowledge of it or any interest. It is of course possible that the captured equipment was too much damaged to disclose much. They were aware from monitoring that we used centimetric ground radar but did not apparently know of its use for fire control.

SECTION B

Report on Technical Work in Progress at the E.L.I.

Introduction

The E.L.I., together with about 10 other similar research institutes was formed at the end of 1943. The formation of these institutes was precipitated by the examination of a captured H2S Mark II equipment (Rotterdam) which appears to have greatly surprised the German radar designers and users by its numerous novel features namely, the centimetre technique, the short pulse technique, and the PPI presentation. The German radar authorities were rudely awakened to the fact that the confidence they had placed in the technical superiority of their own equipment was totally unjustified. A belated and desperate effort has been made to bring German radar technique up to date, but this could only be done in a scattered, piecemeal fashion since the Allied bombing had apparently forbidden the formation of a single, or even a few large establishments.

The technical work described below shows all the hallmarks of a desperate attempt to cover in a short time a wide field of research and development with no clear view of the major objectives, with no concerted development of any single technique on an adequate scale, and with single small establishments attempting to cover numerous aspects of H2S techniques and even attempting to advance beyond the known English and American techniques before these had been completely mastered. In general, the progress has been slow due to numerous dislocations of the work and also because too ambitious a programme seems to have been undertaken. No technical progress has been made in the last two or three months owing to the dislocation resulting from the transfer from Reichenau to Plansee.

All the problems investigated at E.L.I. were presented to the institute in a more or less defined form and although the purpose for which the development work was to be used was well known to the investigators at the E.L.I., the decision to utilise a particular technique for a particular project was made by the central controlling organisation (BHF). This organisation divided up a particular project into its component problems and submitted the individual problems to a number of establishments of which the E.L.I. was one.

1. (a) 3 cm. Radar Equipment

An experimental two mirror system (separate T and R) has been set up to make general studies of the operation of equipment at this wavelength. The cm. technique was very crude. The antenna consisted of two fixed mirrors about 24 in. dia., rear fed, with a simple reflector plate at the mouth of the wave guide used to illuminate the mirror. The modulator, a rough copy of that used in

H2S equipment (triggered spark gap), was used to drive a LMS 12 magnetron mounted in an electro-magnet. A simple crystal receiver which was a copy of an earlier British design was mounted directly behind the receiving mirror. Judging by the proximity of the receiving and transmitting mirrors, the crystal (pyrites) must either have been almost completely burned out or else of so low an initial sensitivity as to make it robust (the figure given for burnout level was 800 milliwatt to one watt for 1 microsec. pulses). The construction of the crystal confirmed this indication since it consisted of a loop of tungsten wire with one end in contact with pyrites and must have had a very large contact capacity.

The 3rd harmonic of a 9 cm. magnetron was used for mixing owing to the short life (about two hours) of the German 3 cm oscillator, an attempted copy of the U.S. 723A. No techniques were available for measuring receiver sensitivity nor did there seem to be a clear appreciation of the relevent factors. The unnumbered report, Vorlaufige Unterlagen des Gerates Rax I, gives circuit diagrams and some indications of the performance of the equipment. E.L.I. Bericht No.8/1 gives details of modulator, magnet, transmitter output circuit, and a description of a simple power monitoring device. In the present site the equipment is directed straight at a mountain side some two miles away and rising to some 5000 feet above the level of the equipment. No smaller targets had yet been investigated. Photographs of the equipment and the target have been taken.

Accurate measuring technique for determining the performance of radar equipment at centimetre wavelengths was almost non-existent. There was clearly only the faintest glimmerings of the knowledge of such problems as mode changing, spectrum, pulling, frequency selectivity of antenna system, and the quantative significance of magnetron matching. There was no knowledge at all, even by hearsay, of such factors as spike burnout of crystals, crystal conversion gain and temperature, i.f. noise factor, etc. No techniques were available for absolute receiver measurements nor was there any knowledge of such equipment elsewhere. Estimates of the crystal receiver performance were not considered accurate to better than about six or ten db. Generally the 3 cm. technique was equivalent to that current in the U.K. and U.S. at the end of 1941.

(b) <u>0.8 cm Equipment</u>

A 0.8 cm. echelon-strapped magnetron with electro-magnet (4500 gauss) and 1 microsec, 400 pps modulator was being set up with the object of building a similar set to that being worked at 3 cm. The magnetron, LMS 14, had an input of 100 kw and 1 to 3 kw output. Nothing was known about the spectrum and stability of the magnetron and this was not surprising since there was only a vague knowledge of the mode change problem at the longer wavelengths.

(c) No development of valves was carried out at the E.L.I. and the supply of valves to E.L.I. by the B.H.F. was so meagre as to indicate the use of inferior techniques, e.g. harmonic mixing for receivers. Much of the information regarding valve performance was obtained from external sources, (the valve manufacturer, generally Telefunken, or B.H.F.) One puzzling piece of information of this sort which was constantly referred to was the statement that the starting up time of the German magnetron in use was of the order of one half to one microsec. No explanation was given of this phenomenon nor had any confirmation been made at E.L.I. itself.

(d) A device was used for measuring the transitter power which involved a resistive wire across the guide, heated by the r.f. power, exciting a photoelectric cell. The accuracy claimed was about 20%, but no explanation was given for the choice of a photoelectric cell rather than a measurement of resistance change. The device was d.c. calibrated and the calibration was used without any correction.

2. (a) I.F. Amplifier Studies (Dr. Harmans)

Mathematical studies were being made of the optimum tuning and Q of the stages of a multistage i.f. amplifier consisting of single tuned circuits each tuned to a different frequency. A simple graphical method had been worked out for evaluating the alleged optimum tuning and Q's of the circuits to give maximum gain for a given number of stages. It was claimed that theoretically at least results of such a computation would give a better gain than staggered pairs or triple and double-tuned circuits and as good a gain as a negative feedback amplifier. Problems such as the dependence of the amplifier gain and bandwidth on tube characteristics or the effect of variable gain control had only been given a cursory examination, nor had the question of the practicability and reproducibility of such a system in manufacture been given much consideration. No experimental investigation of the transient response with varying signal amplitude and pulse width had been made, although some calculations of the group velocity through the system had been made. There was no familiarity with the problem of i.f. noise factor and the only reasons given for choosing a particular noise i.f. frequency in a particular case were considerations of the design of the amplifier itself. The work up to date is reported in Bericht No.4 of E.L.I. December 1944.

(b) Pulse Forming Networks using Coupled Inductances
(Dr. Harmans)

Pulse forming networks using coupled inductances were being investigated as a means of reducing the number of elements required to give a rectangular pulse of a certain quality. The coupling was controlled by the design and spacing of the inductances. It was claimed that a network with two stages could, by this technique, be designed to give as good a one microsec. pulse as the previously used six section network similar to that used in the H2S equipment. A network of this type had been made experimentally and was operating but it was difficult to check the claims made for it since the scope used for examining the pulse had a maximum speed of 40 microsec across the diameter. It was alleged that although the total capacity requires in such a network is greater than in a simple network, the resulting arrangement is smaller and simpler to make.

3. (a) A 'fast' time base A scope was being developed which would give a maximum speed of 1.6 cm per microsec. The sweep was approximately linear being part of an exponential curve. The circuit technique in general was very elementary and apparently no standard test equipment of this sort was obtainable from external sources. Details in E.L.I. Ber. No. 7th Jan. 1945.

(b) Equipment was being developed to provide a standard design for a pulse generator producing pulses of between .1 to 3 microsec., 0 to 100 volts amplitude, 50 cyc. to 200 Kc rep. rate. A standard oscillator covering 50 cyc. to 200 Kc. was necessary to drive the pulse generator. The technique is crude and direct viz. amplification of the incoming sine wave, drastic limiting, differentiating, further limiting. Phase shifting of the sine wave is used and pulse width is changed by changing differentiating time constants. Technique similar to that used in 1940 for A.I. Mark 7. Work reported in E.L.I. Bericht No.9. In one arrangement calibration pips were provided by mixing the third harmonic of a 100 Kc oscillator with the fundamental. The mixture producing sharp pips for calibrating times bases (Ber.No.7).

4. Test had been made of German copies of U.S. 715A modulator tube (obtained from captured AN/APS-15 equipment (Meddo) and the general opinion was expressed that these tubes greatly surpassed triodes of German design that had previously been used in magnetron modulators. Some tests had also been made of the use of a saturated diode in series with the magnetron in order partly to compensate for the low differential impedance of the magnetron. These tests had been discontinued since the improvement in current stability of the magnetron saturated diode combination was not considered to be worth while in view of the practical complications involved by the introduction of the diode.

5. Counter Window and Jamming Devices

From 1943 onwards a whole series of modifications to standard radar equipment has been successively developed, all based on the same fundamental principle, that is, the utilisation of the phase of the received pulse from a system in which the transmitter phase is controlled in a coherent manner.

5. (a) **Wurzlaus**

The Wurzlaus system was developed by Dr. Ing. Fack and Prof. Muller of the Max Wien Institute in Hamburg as an immediate measure against window and was first used in 1943. The technique is straight forward. A c.w. cohering oscillator is used in order to regulate accurately the starting phase of the transmitter. The received signal is mixed with this oscillator and if the target is stationary the phase relation between the coherent oscillator and the signal is constant resulting in a pulse of constant shape. For moving targets the phase relation is shifting rapidly so that a blurred pulse, that is a Laus (louse), is obtained. Since the coherent oscillator is running continuously care must be taken to prevent it jamming the receiver. This means accurate regulation of the amount of coherent oscillator used. To minimise these difficulties, the coherent oscillator was set at a freq. 500 kc different from the transmitter in which case the pulses from stationary and moving targets look like this:

Stationary target   Moving target

The main difficulties experienced in this system were (a) the use of a c.w. oscillator near the transmitting frequency, (b) the elaborate manipulation necessary when changing transmitter frequency, i.e. the tuning of the local oscillator and the tuning and accurate power level adjustment of the coherent oscillator. To overcome these difficulties Tastlaus was developed.

(b) **Tastlaus**

This system was developed by Dr. Pohlmann of the RLM and was first used around the end of 1944. In this system the coherent oscillator is at i.f. freq., and is only mixed with the local oscillator for a period sufficient to cover the transmitted pulse. This allows a much greater latitude in the amount of cohering oscillator permitted and simplifies the process of shifting frequency so that this process is in fact no more difficult than with a simple radar set. In actual practice the system is a little more complicated since two i.f. frequencies are used in succession in the Wurzburg equipment and the coherent oscillator frequency corresponds to that of the second i.f. freq.

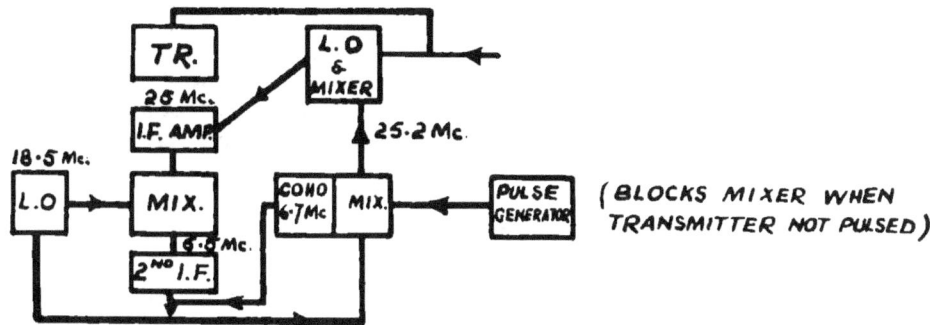

Block Diagram of Tastlaus as Fitted to Wurzburg Radars.

In both the Wurzlaus and Tastlaus the freq. of the coherent oscillator is not set exactly at the transmitter freq., but at a freq. of a few hundred Kc different. Apart from the reasons given in 5(a), this arrangement has an additional advantage that a stationary target gives a characteristic wiggle and not a straight topped pulse and a moving target gives a completely blurred blob and not a rapidly varying pulse shape. This probably makes the discrimination between moving and fixed targets simpler.

(c) Windlaus

Wurzlaus and Tastlaus are only successful against window jamming when the radial velocity of the window cloud is negligible. To overcome this limitation a modification of Tastlaus known as Windlaus was developed in which an audio-freq. corresponding to the doppler freq. of the window was fed into the second i.f. mixer and adjusted in both phase and amplitude so as to cancel out the window echo.

(d) Schiebelaus

In the Windlaus, two controls are necessary, amplitude and phase, in order to cancel the doppler beat of the window. In the system, Schiebelaus, now being developed at the E.L.I., a single control only is necessary corresponding to the radial velocity of the window. This system is similar to Wurzlaus with the addition of a r-f phase goniometer which can be driven by a motor at a speed corresponding to the window radial velocity. It suffers from all the disadvantages of Wurzlaus except the disturbance due to the radial velocity of the window cloud.

(e) Reisslaus

This is an attempt to combine the advantages of Tastlaus and Schiebelaus, namely the simplification of tuning of Tastlaus and the elimination of window doppler beating as in Schiebelaus. The method used is to change the frequency of the cohering oscillator for a few microsecs between each transmitted pulse. The amplitude of the pulse producing the freq. shift is varied in a linear fashion to correspond to the radial velocity of the window, it being assumed that the degree of freq. shifting is proportional to the amplitude of the pulse producing freq. shift. The linear sawtooth which is used to control the amplitude of the freq. changing pulse is arranged so as to correspond to 360 degree change in phase for each cycle of the sawtooth. The operator controls the slope of the sawtooth and the remainder of the equipment is the same as Tastlaus.

The development of these anti-jamming systems is usually done by first setting up a model system using a supersonic tank and replacing the r.f. transmitter by a supersonic transmitter at about 7 Mc.

(f) <u>A comprehensive anti-jamming system</u>

A system is being developed which is designed to eliminate window jamming, pulse jamming and c.w. jamming and to provide a very large factor of improvement with noise jamming at the expense of a corresponding increase in the effective time constant of the system. A full description of this system together with some results obtained with a model system using 7 Mc. supersonics in place of r.f. are given in Vorschlag No.2, <u>Vorschlage und Modellversuche zur Entstorung von Funkmessgeraten durch hochfrequenten Phasenvergleich,</u> of the E.L.I.

The system consists of a combination of a number of different principles, (a) the use of a coherent oscillator as in Tast-laus, (b) the use of a supersonic delay line with a delay accurately equal to and in fact controlling the pulse repetition rate in order to compare in both amplitude and phase successive pulses, (c) the use of a phase sensitive rectifier bridge to compare each pulse with the successive pulse, (d) an integration of the output from the phase bridge over a time corresponding to about ten pulse intervals (about 1/400th of a second), which corresponds to the use of an i.f. band width of 400 cycles, (e) the deliberate phase shifting of alternate pairs of pulses so as to provide an effective modulation of any incoming c.w. signal, but by providing a polarity switching at a corresponding freq. to the output of the bridge, the echoes from genuine targets are not disturbed by this phase shifting, (f) a simple static phase shift in one of the incoming channels of the bridge can be used so as to arrange for a complete cancellation to correspond to any constant velocity of a window cloud.

In order to provide an indication of range to the genuine target, a slowly moving strobe of width approximately equal to the pulse width is used and the speed of the strobe is such that about ten pulses are received during the passage of the strobe from one end of the the received pulse from a target to the other. The

The speed of the strobe can be controlled manually and ganged with this control is a corresponding adjustment of the integration time constant of the output from the bridge. The long time constant of the system makes it impractical for all-round search and of course also for PPI presentation, but it may well be of some value for GL where the rate at which information is obtained might be sufficient.

The use of the coherent oscillator provides the normal protection against window and random pulse jamming; the integration of the phase coherent amplitudes of successive pulses provides the improved noise factor (claimed to be about 35 db signal to noise improvement, that is the ratio of 400 cycles to 1 mc.); the phase switching of the transmitter and the bridge output provides the protection against c.w, although unless the c.w. jammer was accurately stable in frequency over a period of 1/400th of a second, the c.w. could be regarded as having random phase and the switching would merely provide additional protection against c.w. Of course the system provides no protection against c.w. signals which saturate the receiver nor against a jammer which was coherent in phase with the transmitted pulse.

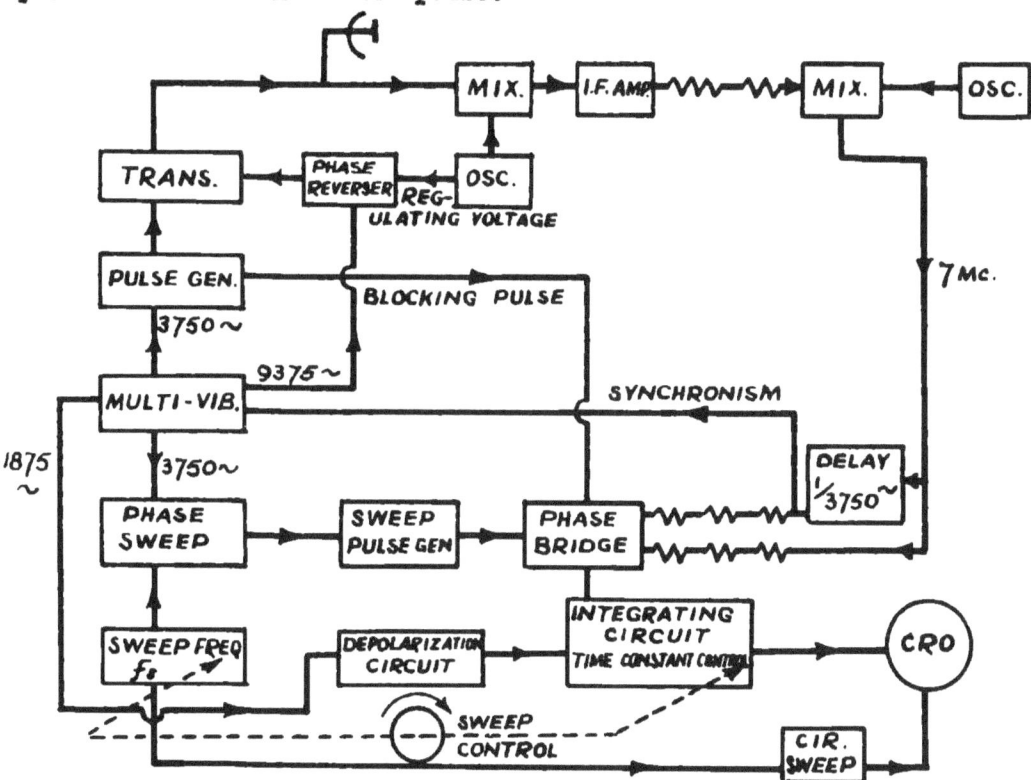

A block schematic of a simplified version of the arrangement shown in Tafel 4 of the report is given above.

6. The Reutte extension of the Institute

Two laboratories and a store room were on the upper floor of a mill in Reutte. The work in hand there was (a) an F.M. method of measuring the error in range of a shell splash (Litzer) and (b) the development of a thermal method of detecting millimetric waves (Drs. Gotz and Sollmann).

(a) The F.M. method of measuring range differences was begun on request from the BHF in Sept. 1944, to develop the particular method for application to the Seetakt radar. The staff concerned were far from satisfied that this was the best approach to the problem and would, if given the choice, have preferred to use a PPI display. It would seem that the instruction to proceed on F.M. lines was in the hope of obtaining a modification for Seetakt. The staff knew nothing of the operational requirements and were approaching the problem on purely academic lines. The radar was again simulated by a delay tank using quartz oscillators in water for transmitter and receiver, and a jet of air to represent the burst.

The freq. ranges used were selected on the basis of the target being between 1 and 20 km. and the splash displacement required to be measured being between 25 metres and 1 km. It was assumed that the lowest freq. difference that could be used was 50 c.p.s. which gives a range of Δf of 50 to 2000 c.p.s. A condenser rotating at about 4 c.p.s. comprised part of the selector circuit for this freq. range and relays were arranged to stop the rotation as soon as a signal was received. It was admitted that the method would be useless if two tagets were in the beam at once but some thought had been given to the obvious difficulties of determining whether the splash displacement was positive or negative and of determining errors in angle as well as in time.

To determine whether the splash displacement was positive or negative a complicated arrangement of D.C. amplifiers and relays had been worked out and set up in bread-board form. The principle was to correct the two freq. differences obtained from target and splash into amplitude differences and to compare the two amplitude differences. After D.C. amplification, relays were arranged to give visual + and − signals.

No circuits had been worked out for determining errors in angle but the proposal was to use some form of freq. modulation synchronised with the sweep in bearing.

No practical trials with actual shell splashes had been carried out and Dr. Plendl knew of no such trials at Peenemunde or elsewhere. No thought appeared to have been given to the use of such an F.M. apparatus alongside the radar but the general idea seemed to be to use the Seetakt radar for target laying and the F.M. apparatus for splash errors.

Two reports completed so far (Lehn-bericht No.19 and 20) are being forwarded to CIOS. These include photographs and circuit diagrams.

The story of this project might well be regarded as an example of how not to handle a project.

(b) <u>The thermal method of detecting millimetric waves</u> is a development of Dr. Czerny's original work on infra-red detection (described in Z.f.Phys. Bd.77, Heft 9 and 10, 1932; Bd.108, Heft 1 and 2, 1937). On to thin membranes, prepared from cellulose varnish and about .1 to .2 μ thick, are sputtered silver or bismuth dipoles about 2 μ thick, and a half wavelength long. The dipole or dipoles are obtained by covering the membrane with a slotted plate during the sputtering process. The resistance of the dipoles is between 70 and 100 ohms. A thin paraffin oil film is evaporated on to the membrane which is then supported in vacuo at the focus of the receiving mirror. Any radiation falling on the mirror then heats the dipole and causes evaporation of the paraffin oil at the current nodes. By viewing the membrane with parallel light the interference cloud produced by the oil film will therefore change to white at the current nodes.

The work is at present being done on Xband and some results have been obtained on 1.5 cms. It is proposed later to use .9 cm, the transmitter for which is already available.

The ultimate aim of such work is to produce at the focus of the mirror a representation of the target without scanning. A mosaic of dipoles would be needed and work on a mosaic has already started. The obvious difficulties are lack of resolution owing to mutual interaction between dipoles together with poor sensitivity and inability to obtain quantitative results. As regards sensitivity, reflections have been detected from a 10 by 10 cms metal plate at a distance of 10 metres using about 5 Kw at 400 c.p.s., 1 μ-s.

A report (Labor-bericht No.21) giving sketches of the appearance of the membrane and dipoles is being forwarded.

SECTION C

PERSONNEL OF THE ERNST LECHER INSTITUTE

Reutte, 10, Mai 1945

Name (No.8s)	Qualification	Place of Birth	Date of Birth	Subjects in which specialising
Dr.Plendl	Dipl.Phys.	Munchen	1900	Navigation (fruher); Wellen ausbreitung, Antennen, Funkmesstechnik (Schuler von Senneck).
Dr.Herzog	Dipl.Phys.	Zweibrucken	1909	Navigation (fruher); Funkmes technik, Untersuchungen im cm-Gebiet(Allgem.) (Sch.V.Zenneck)
Dr.Owczarek				a.d.Institut ausgeschieden Funkmesstechnik im cm-Geb.
Dr.Klages	Dipl.Phys.	Holmunden	1915	Antennen fur cm-Wellen, Dipoltheorie, Kristallphysik (Sch.v.Debye)
Scheiringer	Ing.	Wien	1906	Allgem.Hochfrequenzmesstechnik,Parabolspiegel fur cm-Gebiet, cm-Sender.
Steinbrecher	Dipl.Ing.	Melk	1919	Anpassungsfragen bei Hohlleiterkombinationen
Gangl	Dipl.Ing.	Aussig	1907	Schlitzantennen
Schult	Dipl.Ing.	Hamburg	1912	Dielektrische Antennen, Messleitungen im dm-Gebiet
Dr.Harmans	Dipl.Phys.	Dresden	1912	Impulstechnik,Breitband verstarker (Sch.v. Waldhausen)

Name (No.8s)	Qualification	Place of Birth	Date of Birth	Subjects in which specialising
Alfke	Dipl.Phys.	Delitzch	1914	Impulstechnik,Tastung von Hochleistungssendern
Weckerle	Ing.	Karlsruhe	1914	Impulstechnik
Dr.Ronnberg	Dipl.Phys.	Rostock	1913	Funkmesstechnik; Rauschuntersuchungen an Empfangern.
Reiger	cand.phys	Lindau	1920	cm-Funkmesstechnik (sender und Empfanger)
Dr.Zschirnt	Dipl.Phys.	Dusseldorf	1911	Ultraschall;Funkmesstechnik und Navigation (fruher) (Sch.v. Zenneck)
Huter	Dipl.Phys.	Baden-Baden	1917	Ultraschall Funkmesstechnik und Navigation (fruher)
Schumacher	Dipl.Ing.	Waldbrol	1910	Ultraschall
Peersmann	Ing.	Hamburg	1911	Niederfrequenztechnik, Funkmesstechnik.
Donn	Dipl.Ing.	Halle	1908	Allgem. Niederfrequenstechnik und Impulstastung
Dr.Titze	Dipl.Ing.	Potsdam	1903	Niederfrequenzauswertung.
Dr.K.H. Schwarz	Dipl.Phys.			allgem.Niederfrequenstechnik, Impulstechnik, Empfanger fur UKW und dm-Technik.
Dr.Gotz	Dipl.Phys.	Wien	1901	allgem.Physik und Optik
Sollmann	Stud.Rat	Breslau	1913	allgem.Physik, Hochvakuumtechnik.

Name (No.8s)	Qualification	Place of Birth	Date of Birth	Subjects in which specialising
Dr.Hadwiger	Stud.Rat	Wien	1908	Mathematik und allgem. Physik
Dr.Hofmann	Chemiker			
Huber	Dipl.Ing.			Chemie und Hochvakuumtechnik.
Dr.W.Schwarz	Dipl.Phys.			Rohrentechnik (gasgefullte Rohren)
Dr.Horstmann	Stud.Rat.	Erfurt	1908	Antennen und Rukstrahlphysik
Dr.Ulm	Dozent	Gelsenkirchen	1908	Mathematik, Impuls-und Laufzeitketten
Gerger				Mathematik, Impulstechnik und Ultraschall

SECTION D

List of Reports, Memorandums etc. Prepared by the Staff of the Ernst Lecher Institute

ENDBERICHTE

Bericht Nr.:	Title	Bearbeiter	Abt.	Datum	Geh.Nr.
1	Zum Aufbau von Dipolreihen und Dipolgruppen als Langsstrahler	Horstmann	2	20.1.44	71/44g
2	Impulsgenerator I	Weckerle	2	1.8.44	
3	Wellenmesser fur cm-Wellen	Neitzel	2	30.12.44	
4	Ein Beitrag zum Problem des Breitbandverstarkers	Harmans	2	20.12.44	
5	Beschreibung eines Messplattes fur Hohlleiter	Steinbrecher	2	9.12.44	
6	Drehzahlregelung eines Motors durch einen Schwebungssummer	Peersmann	1	6.1.45	14/45g
7	Impulsbreitenmesser	Bernhardt/ Schwarz	1	25.1.45	
8	Funkmessgerat fur cm-Wellen. Teil I Sender mit Tastgerat	Harmans/ Reiger	2	31.1.45	
9	Impulsgenerator mit veranderlicher Bandbreite	Weckerle	2	18.1.45	
10	Experimentelle Untersuchungen an einem Langsstrahler aus 3 gespeisten Dipolen	Renz	1	15.1.45	
11	Uber den Storeinfluss der h-Wellen bei der Widerstandsmessung eines Querschlitzes im Hohlrohr unter Verwendung der E-Welle.	Klages	1	20.2.45	

Bericht Nr:	Title	Bearbeiter	Abt.	Datum	Geh.Nr.
12	Der dielektrische Leiter mit rechteckigem Querschnitt	Klages/ Fiedler	1	24.2.45	128/45
13	Das Rechteckloch in der Hohlleiterwand als Stuck einer homogenen gedampften Leitung	Klages/ Otto	1	3.3.45	129/45g

L A B O R - B E R I C H T E

Bericht Nr.:	Title	Bearbeiter	Abt	Datum	Geh.Nt.
1	Messungen and Versuchdetektoren	Reiger	2	8.8.44	
1a	Anlage z.Schreiben über den stand der Arbeiten am Forschungsauftrag SS 4948-6139 6941/44 Arbeitsweisse Des Gerates	Owczarek	2	31.7.44	
2	Wellenmesser fur cm-Wellen	Neitzel	2	14.10.44	
3	Das Auflosungsvermogen der Strahlung v.Sendern mit periodisch veranderlicher Frequenz f.d.Ortung von Aufschlagen beim Beschuss Beweglicher Ziele	Titze	1	20.10.44	
4	Stand der Arbeiten am kunstlichen, auf elektrischer Basis erzeugten Rundortungsbild	Waltel	2	28.10.44	
5	Bericht uber Messungen in Holleitungen	Steinbrecher	2	28.10.44	
5a	Untersuchung des Uberganges einer konzentrischen Leitung in eine Hohlleitung	Steinbrecher	2	4.11.44	
6	Jmpuls-Sendeanlage	Donn/Muller	1	30.10.44	
7	Jmpulsbreitenmesser	Bernhardt/Schwarz	1	30.10.44	
8	Kurzbericht uber d. Stand d. Arbeiten betr. Tourenzahlregelung eines Motors durch einen Schwebungssummer	Peersmann	1	6.11.44	245/44g

Bericht Nr.:	Title	Bearbeiter	Abt	Datum	Geh.Nt.
9	Erhohung d.Peilgenaugkeit bei Verwendung v.zwei mit versch.Frequenzen modulierten Sendern unter Ausnutzung d.Schwebung d. beiden Modulationsfrequenzen	Titze	1	28.11.44	
10	Bisherige Arbeiten am 3 cm-Empfanger	Reiger	2	21.12.44	309/44g
11	Einfluss d.Oberflachen von Tripelspiegeln auf ihre Reflexionsfahigkeit	Owczarek	2	28.12.44	
12	Leistungsmesser fur cm-Jmpulssender	Reiger	2	29.12.44	
13	Zum elektrischen Verhalten eines Schlitzes in der Wandung eines rechteckigen Hohlrohres bei Anregung der E-Welle	Klages	1	30.12.44	15/45 g.
14	Auswertung eines "Meddo"-Beutebildes "Munchen"	Krober	3	20.11.44	
15	Experimentelle Untersuchngen zur Hohlrohrangregung eines Rotationsparabolspiegels mit Reflexionsscheibe	Klages/ Scheiringer	1	19.1.45	13/45 g.
16	Voruntersuchung uber das Lei-Ronnberg tendmachen einer Ballonoberflache	Ronnberg	2	19.1.45	37/45 g.
17	Tastung von Magnetfeldrohren	Alfke	2	23.1.45	
18	Jmpulsstabilisierung durch gesattigte Dioden	Reiger	2	26.1.45	

Bericht Nr.:	Title	Bearbeiter	Abt	Datum	Geh.Nr.
19	Niederfrequenzseitige Anordnung zum Messen des Abstandes zweier Punkte im Raum bei Verwendung frequenzveränderlicher Sender	Titzer	1	14.2.45	
20	Niederfrequenzeitige Anordnung zur Feststellung des Vorzeichens der gegenseitigen Lage zweier Punkte im Raum bei Verwendung Frequenzveränderlicher Sender	Titzer	1	15.2.45	
21	Verfahren zur Sichtbarmachg. sehr kurzer elektrischer Wellen	Sollmann	2	28.2.45	
22	Entwicklung und stand der Arbeiten zur Herstellung von Vakuumthermoelementen mit Dipolen zum Empfang von cm-und mm-Wellen	Huber	2	26.2.45	
23	Der Einfluss der Rauhigkeit der Oberfläche eines Parabolspiegels auf die Verstärkung bei cm-Wellen	Scheiringer	1	1.3.45	
24	Zur Stabilität von Magnetfeldröhen	Reiger	2	12.3.45	
25	Zur Mehrwelligkeit von Magnetfeldröhren	Reiger	2	13.3.45	

Z W I S C H E N B E R I C H T E

1	Der Kugelballon als Ruckkstrahlnormal	Ronnberg	2	1.3.45	

Bericht Nr.:	Title	Bearbeiter	Abt	Datum	Geh.Nr.

VORSCHLAGE

1	Selbsttatige Abschusseinrichtung fur die Bekamfpung von Zielen mit hoher Geschwindigkoit	Peersmann	1	30.10.44	234/44 g
2	Vorschlage und Modellversuche zur Entstorung von Funkmessgeraten durch hohen frequenten Phasenvergleich	Zschirnt	1	26.2.45	

VORTRAGE

1	Die verschiedenen Moglichkeiten der Jmpulserzeugung	Owozarek	2	8.10.44	

ZUSAMMENSTELLUNG

1	Reichweiten-Formeln fur Funkmessgerate	Horstmann		29.12.44	
2	Uber elektr.(tg δ ; ε) bezw opt.(η ; η x) Eigenschaften von flussegen und festen Stoffen im Bereich von λ = 100 μ bis 10 cm	Gotz	2	.45	

ABHANDLUNGEN

Nr. 888	Title	Bearbeiter	Abt.	Datum	Geh.Nr.
1	Stielstrahler-Gruppen	Horstmann	1	25.10.44	
2	Abschatzung uber die Moglichkeit, den Mond funkmesstechnisch zu erfassen	Reiger	2	28.10.44	
3	Vergleichend Betrachtung uber Parabolspiegel und Spharische Linsen im Beriich kurzer elektrischer Wellen (cm.mm)	Gotz	2	13.12.44	
4	Bemerkungen zur Theorie der Lochantennen	Horstmann	1	2.1.45	
5	Darstellung und Anwendungen derTheorie derBeugung elekstromagnetischer Wellen von Stratton und Chu	Horstmann	1		

List of reports etc. prepared by the Institute and removed for transmission to C.I.O.S.

Bericht No. 4.   Ein Beitrag zum Problem des Breitbandverstärkers.

    " " 8/I. Funkmessgerät für cm-Wellen (Sender mit Tastgerät)

    " " 7. Impulsebreitmesser

Labor-bericht 19 and 20.   Anordung zur Feststellung des Vorzeichens der gegenseitigen Lage zweier Punkte im Raum.

Labor-bericht 21.   Verfahren zur Sichtbarmachung Sehr kurzer electrischer Wellen.

Vorschlag No.2.   Entstörung von Funkmessgeräten durch hochfrequenten Phasenvergleich.

Circuit Diagrams - Vorläufiger Unterlagen des Gerätes Rax I.

Section F.

    This list is being retained by the investigating team.

SECTION "G"

REPORTS REMOVED FROM ERNST LECHER INSTITUTE

1. Forschungs Bericht 1922 Feb. 9, 1945 Ferdinand Braun Inst. Inves

2. Forschungs Bericht No. 1916 Mar. 25, 1944 Kommando der flak forsuchsteele Karlshagen.

3. Forschungs Bericht No. 1963 Feb. 9, 1944 Flakvorsuchtstelle der Luftwaffe Karlshagen/Pommern

4. Forschungs Bericht No. 1853 Sept. 1943, Flugfunkforschung Inst. Oberphaffenhoffen

5. Versuchtsbericht No. 6 No. 1, 1944 Zentralvorsuhstelle der hf. Ulm Dornstadt

6. Forschungsbericht No. 1920 April 20, 1944 Ernst Orlich Inst. Danzig/langfuhr

7. Untersuch ungen und Mitteilungen No. 767 May 5, 1944 Deutscher-Forschungsanstalt fur Seigelflug, Ernst Udet Ainring

8. Forschungsbericht No. 2022 Dec. 13, 1944 Max Wien Inst. Hamburg.

9. Forschungsbericht No. 1785 June 15, 1943 Inst. Fur Electro Physic der Deutschen vorsuchanstalten fur Luftfahrt. Berlin/Adlerhof

10. Forschungsbericht No. 1635 June 20, 1942 Inst. fur Bildwesen der Deutschenvorsuchanstalt fur Luftfahrt, Berlin/Alderhof

11. Forschungsbericht No. 1997 May 3, 1943, Inst. fur Bildwesen der Deuschenvorsuchanstalten fur Luftrahrt.

12. Forschungsbericht No. 1755 Mar. 1, 1943 Optisches Inst. T.M.S. Berlin.

13. Forschungsbericht No. 1695/2 May 1943 Phy. Int. T.H.S. München.

14. Forschungsbericht No. 1890 Jan. 5, 1944 Theor. Phy. Inst. Univ. Jena

15. Untersuchungen und Mitteilungen No. 837 Nov. 1944 Theo. Phy Inst. Univ. Jena.

16. Forschungsbericht No. 1814 June 26, 1942 Labor. fur H.F. Tech. und Electro Medicin Berlin/Lankwitz

17. Forschungsbericht No. 2018 August 26, 1944 Vier Jahres Inst. fur Schwingungsforschung Berlin (Fassbender).

18. Forschungsbericht No. 1995 Oct. 20, 1944 Vier Jahres Plan Int. fur Schwing. Berlin.

19. Forschungsbericht 1914 Feb. 1944 Funkstrahl Gessellschaft fur Nachrichtentechnik. Berlin.

20. Forschungsbericht No. 1888 Dec. 6, 1943 Flugfunkforschungs Inst. Oberphaffenhofen Aussenstelle Grafelfing

21. Untersuchugen and Mitteilungen No. 4015 August, 11, 1944 FFO Omni-directional antennas for aircraft at 1.9 meters.

22. Forschungsbricht No. 1886 Nov. 26, 1943 Deutsche Forsch. Anst. for Siegelflug Ernst Udet in Conjunction with FFO

23. Forschungsbericht No. 1845 1943 FFO Munchen Aus. Grafelfing Ernst Udet, Inst.

SECTION "H"

Financial position of the Institute, Attitude of the staff etc.

The staff, now about 80, are still at work and are anxious to be allowed to continue. When they evacuated from Reichenau, the Institute received sufficient cash (presumably from the B.H.F.), to cover salaries until the end of June and Dr.Plendl was informed by the investigating team that there was no reason why work should not continue until further instructions were received, or their financial resources were expended. In general no comments were passed on the work going on, but Dr. Plendl was informed that if he was in a position to continue for a while, the projects of most interest were the thermal detection of millimeter waves, and the phase bridge integrating systems, while the work on the FM method of shell splash ranging was a waste of time.

The whole staff were very cooperative and anxious to give demonstrations and the fullest explanations. Dr. Häter, a member of the institute who had worked on physics in the U.S., was very valuable in interpreting. All the labs, workshops, storerooms were inspected. Dr. Plendl's collection of reports from the Institute, was examined and a number of reports (see section g), removed for their general technical interest.

No equipment was removed.

Military Government in Reutte, had no objection to the staff continuing at work. The guard at the Seespitz Hotel is part of the road patrol along Plansee, and will continue as long as the road is patrolled.

REPORT II

INTERROGATION OF DR. PLENDL ON R.C.M.

Date. 21st May 1945

Investigator: S/L Parvis, T.R.E., CIOS Group 1.

Personnel Interviewed: Dr. Plendl and Dr. Häter, of the Ernst Lecher Institute, Plannsee. These personnel had been brought to Munich for Interrogation.

The object of the interview was to attempt to discover the effectiveness of British RCM. against the German navigational beam system used during the early years of the war.

Dr. Plendl had been engaged at Rechlin between 1937 and 1939 on investigations and development of general navigation systems for use by aircraft. (From another interview with Telefunken, later it appeared that Plendl's tone-frequency navigational aid was dropped in 1939.) Then in 1940, General Udet stated a requirement for a precision target bombing aid, and sought the assistance of Dr. Plendl. It was laid down very definitely that only equipment which would be ready by October 1940 could be considered. Plendl and his staff designed, developed, built, and themselves installed a few Ruffian (70 mc/s) equipments, both on the ground and in the aircraft in this short time, although they admitted that in November, most of the people were out at the stations and aerodromes, keeping the rather experimental equipment serviced. KG. 100 was the bomber group involved. While still trying to keep this X gerät equipment serviceable, they were trying to develop in parallel the Y gerät, which would give them greater target accuracy. Both were allowed to go forward: the Service just accepted what Rechlin gave, having stated their requirements. The experimental station at Koethen was primarily responsible for the later developments of the Y gerät. KG.26 was the bomber group operating the Y equipment.

Plendl seemed very proud of his Y beam, and was anxious to know how long it took the British to discover how it worked. The absence of normal equisignal continuous tone was not really a determining factor - the form of the beam was required on technical grounds (synchronisation) alone, but they later realised its additional assets of security.

The beam was used for automatic flying and was highly successful. There were actually 2 equisignal paths, but the equipment could distinguish between them. The aerial array has been photographed viz o o o o o o o Producing overlapping patterns thus.

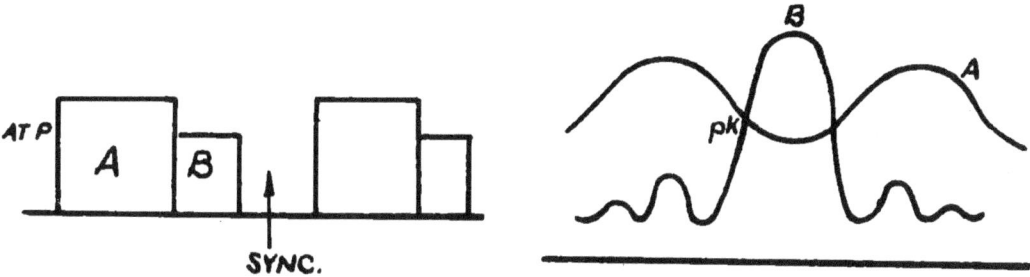

It was stated that each ground station was provided with a Heinrich D/F aerial system and every range measurement was checked before passing instructions to the aircraft.

In spite of the disadvantage of being able to work only one aircraft at a time, the Service officials seemed quite pleased at first with the Y gerät because it gave bombing control to the ground station. Later Plendl was blamed about it being possible to work only one aircraft at a time.

Dr. Plendl made a significant observation about his relations with the Service during the development of the beam systems, in particular the Y system. The whole scheme was worked out at the experimental establishment and completed before handing to the Service for use., The result was that the scientists overlooked such important features as security (i.e. the important part played by the W/T instructions) and the jammability. He implied that if he were developing another system he would bring the Service users in at an early stage of the development so that they could watch such points.

Effects of British Jamming.

The equisignal paths of the 70 mc/s X beams were very much disturbed, and jamming was effective up to about 100 km. from London. The Plymouth area was also bad, up to about 50 km., perhaps more.

The jamming of the Y equipment was effective in spoiling the system, but not so good as the X jamming. They were surprised that we jammed the range rather than the beam, which gave 1/16 accuracy. By a good stroke of luck (for us), the unjammed period of Y operations corresponded to experimental flights by specialist aircraft. Having proved the system, the experts handed over to their trainees, and almost on the first operation with the regular crews, jamming was experienced. The psychological effect was important, and the Luftwaffe (KG.26) always viewed Y with doubt thereafter until a boost was given to the system by the Cherbourg outfit being able to pick up a returning bomber which was in distress, giving it its position, and finally directing it right back to its airfield. The testimony of this crew restored some confidence in the possibilities of the system, but the cat and mouse game was on with the jamming.

Dr. Plendl and Dr. Hüter could not remember all the details: the man who would know best was Dr. Kerzog, who was away sick. They can say definitely however, (because Dr. Hüter was many times helping with the operations at the stations) that their biggest trouble was due to the 300 cps. jamming. As far as Hüter could remember we had not jammed the 3000 cycle tone for a long period. Their method of reading through the jamming when it was not heavy, was to read on the minimum with of the ellipse (which was supposed to close to a straight line). There were two different ground measurement equipments, one by Lorenz, and one by Siemens: Cherbourg had the ellipse presentation, while Kassel had a circular time base and bright spot presentation. The ellipse type was better with jamming.

By the end of April 1941 they were seriously hampered by the jamming. They tried the technique where no warning was given by the W/T but that raised training and operational troubles, and they then reradiated the morse in order to take measurements of range. They tried frequency division arrangements, but it was not very successful because once the receivers in the aircraft was allowed to be returned, the phase calibration went wrong. Finally they devised a method of getting snap readings in 1/10 second.

Without any jamming it took 1 1/2 seconds to take a reading on the ellipse mentod. The measuring accuracy was only claimed to be 300 metres.

Their remembrance was that London was protected effectively, jamming being observed at 50 km. or more. Southampton and Portsmouth were badly jammed areas: Plymouth was jammed, but not so seriously.

They never paid much attention to our jammer positions. They suspected there was a small number on the outskirts of London, and perhaps some near the south coast. No great efforts were made to find exactly where the jammers were, because they had decided it was a hopeless problem trying to destroy them, on the grounds that new jammers would be built elsewhere, which might be worse.

The Y station at Joburg had been photographed by our aircraft and had received 4000 bombs from British aircraft, but it was such a small target that, apart from many craters, the total damage was two people killed.

At the end of 1941, KG.26 and KG.100 were sent to the east and there were practically no planes left with the X or Y equipment, and these bombing aids really ended at the beginning of 1942.

Dr. Plendl's group, with Koethen, later went to the fighter-Y development, which went ahead well. They could not understand why we left it unjammed for so long. Finally "Cigar" (Which they described as Eedle-ee) bothered them a lot. Hüter remembers going to a night fighter control centre which was lavishly equipped place. When Cigar started all the officers had to lay down their phones because of the din. They finally got rid of Cigar jamming by a phase bridge circuit which selected synchronised tones. The 300 cps. tone was dropped out of the fighter Y system, and ambiguities in range were resolved by checking the shift in range when 3000 and 3300 cps. tones were reradiated.

They were quite impressed by the Cigar equipment when they inspected a crashed model. They repaired it and flew it and Hüter liked the panoramic receiver idea very much.

At the end of 1942, Dr. Plendl was given a new job - in charge of the Ernst Lecher Institute, and left navigational systems completely.

S/L Farvis.

ZENTRALVERSUCHSTELLE FUR HOCH FREQUENZ FORSCHUNG (ULM-DORNSTADT)

1. **TARGET NO.** Opportunity

2. **TITLE OF TARGET.** Zentralversuchstelle fur Hochfrequenz Forschung.

3. **LOCATION** Originally at Ulm-Dornstadt but evacuated about the 1st March to the area of Bad Aibling at the following locations:

    (a) Beyharting   (Z 175340) - office and 3 labs.
    (b) Innerthan   (Z 162340) - one laboratory.
    (c) Schalldorf   (Z 239423) - two labs.
    (d) Jakobsburg   (Z 188326) - Chemical lab. in farm buildings.
    (e) Schmidhausen   (Z 191335) - Instruments etc. stores.
    (f) Schlachtcham   (Z 145226) - Workshops.
    (g) Bad Aibling   (Z 19275) - Components store
    (h) Holzhausen   (Z 312395) - Cables and F.M.G. units stored.

4. **INVESTIGATING TEAM.** Comprised some members of C.I.O.S. No.182.

    Lt. Col (acting) R.G.Friend. - Min. of Supply.
    Maj. W.H. Maddison   - Min. of Supply.
    Mr. M.B. Gottlieb   - A.B.L.15.

5. **CONTENTS OF REPORT.**

    Section A: Discussion with Dr.Breuning and general appreciation.
    Section B: Report on technical work in progress and completed.
    Section C: List of personnel.
    Section D: List of reports issued and list of those being forwarded to C.I.O.S.
    Section E: List of scientific personnel in the Bad Aibling area.
    Section F: Action taken.

SECTION A

DISCUSSION WITH DR. BREUNING, DIRECTOR OF Z.H.F. AND GENERAL APPRECIATION.

I. 1. **History of Institute:** The history of this institute seems to have been the outcome of the personal ambition of Dr. Breuning. His previous history seems to have been mainly concerned with investigation of interference with broadcasting. He had worked at various times with the Stuttgart Broadcasting station (1931-32 and 1933-35) the Reichpost (1932-33), and A.E.G. (1935-36). He then joined the Air Ministry for development of navigational aids for the Luftwaffe and Luft Hansa. During the earlier part of the war he was a technical officer (Flt. Oberstabsingenieur) in the Luftwaffe until in 1943 he obtained permission to leave the Luftwaffe to start a research institution as a private venture. Apparently he was backed financially by the Reichstadt Baukhaus, Ulm, the principal (name not quoted) of which was also a high official of the Luftwaffe.

I. 2. The name of the institution when first formed was Hochfrequenz Forschung fur Dr. Breuning. He seems to have sought research projects from the Luftwaffe and Dr. Plendl of B.H.F. without success. When Dr. Esau took over the B.H.F. he showed no more interest in Breuning's Institute but suggested instead that he should take charge of an existing institute at Gatow. This he did for a short while but later (1944) moved this institute to the Ulm-Darnstadt and called the combination the Z.H.F., Ulm-Dornstadt. Apparently he had only minor work to do for about six months, during which period he stated he was training his engineers. He had set up his institute in a disused aerodrome near Dornstadt (it was too small for use by modern aircraft). There were 21 laboratories, which from a subsequent examination would seem to have been well equipped with new instruments as well as a certain amount admitted to have been looted from schools in Holland (including a 5,000 gauss electro magnet which is still at Dornstadt). In March 1944 the B.H.F. took over the financial responsibility for the institute.

2. 1. **Programme.** It proved difficult to obtain a clear statement of the investigations made at the institute. The main problem seems to have been anti-jamming of Freya, Lichtenstein and Wurzburg in common with other establishments. In the case of this establishment there seems to have been little direction from the B.H.F. as to its work. This may explain the many nibbles taken at problems being explored elsewhere. Often the

projects were stated to have been started on the initiative of the institute. On such problems as had been given by the B.H.F. little idea existed as the purpose of the investigations. Significant examples of this were the determinations of polar diagrams of shells and rockets and the measurement of reflection from hot gases etc.

2.2. Other items on the programme were

    (a) a 1,000 Kw modulator for an H2S jammer
    (b) Jamming of H2S
    (c) Reflection measurements from wood, water, absorbing paper, etc.
    (d) Some nebulous attempts to produce synthetic rectifier crystals.
    (e) An ingenious, but improbable, scheme to show the Doppler frequency of an echo.
    (f) a "window" simulator.
    (g) propeller modulation studies.

2.3. In addition to the above items there seemed to be a number of subsidiary developments "sub-contracted" from the main development at other institutes.

3. Present situation.

3.1. On the 20th March it was stated that Hitler issued a general order that all equipment and records were to be destroyed if they were in danger of falling into our hands. Between the 1st March and the 1st April this institute moved from its original location to scattered points in the vicinity of Bad Aibling. Many of the staff who had come to the new locations had left but he still had about 33 engineers and physicists with him. He declared however that he had no means with which to continue paying them and most were anxious to return to their own homes as soon as this would be permitted.

3.2. Subsequent inspection showed that the work had only been restarted on a reduced scale, as many of the crates of equipment had not been reopened after the move and the machines had not been set up in the workshops. Accommodation was scanty and poor, being in rooms in country inns, barns and cowsheds. The various locations were scattered widely in an agricultural area and were somewhat inaccessible. The advent of military occupations had produced the usual amount of damage and looting at Beyharting, Innerthan and Schalldorf. Practically nothing had been reconstructed of the experimental apparatus at these places, in fact at Schalldorf it had been pushed to one side to allow the staff to earn a living by repairing radio receivers, while at Beyharting the contents of one laboratory had been unceremoniously dumped in another to make room for troops quarters.

4.1. **Reports**: The institute had issued 11 interim and 17 final reports, a list and summaries of which is included in this report with a list of those removed for C.I.O.S.

5. **Organisation**: The original organisation is given fully in the C.A.F.T. assessment report on the laboratories at Ulm-Dornstadt. It consisted of four divisions (abteilungen), the three technical divisions being under Maier, Gorke and Volkel and the administrative division under Siewick. The work of Maier's division included anti-jamming work on Y system, A J work on Lichtenstein etc, propeller modulation, window simulator and some odd chemical work including an attempt to make crystals. Gorke's division was responsible for jammers for Rotterdam, reflection measurements and search receivers. Division three under Volkel worked on various improvements to Freya and Wurzburg including A.J. and Doppler work.

6. **Appreciation.**

Dr. Breuning and his staff were very anxious to please and assist in the investigation. In addition to Dr. Breuning the principal people interrogated were Dr. Herrold and Prof. Gorcke. The impression gained was that the latter was the most sound technically of the people we saw. While it is perhaps unfair to judge an organisation so soon after it has been uprooted we feel that this is not perhaps one of the outstanding institutes of the R.H.F. Whether one should blame Dr. Breuning for having allowed the efforts of his staff to be frittered away on improvising and academic schemes or the B.H.F. for having only given odd jobs, is hard to say. Nevertheless the history indicates that Dr. Breuning is ambitious and individualist beyond his capacity while it is evident that Drs. Esau and Plendl were reluctant to support this institute. Breuning asserted twice that he had failed to obtain appointments (as Chief Engineer, Cologne Radio station in 1935 and a teaching appointment) because he was not a member of the Nazi Party. We have no evidence to confirm this statement.

SECTION B.

REPORT ON TECHNICAL WORK OF THE VARIOUS LABORATORIES.

Innerthan laboratory: This laboratory represents the evacuated parts of the Abteilung No.2 of the institute and was under Prof. Dr. Gorcke. This division had covered work on polar diagrams of shells and mortars, or reflections from rocket gases, search receivers and jammers.

The study of <u>polar diagrams of shells and rockets</u> was begun at the request of the B.H.F. in December 1944 but no indication was given to the institute as to reason for operational requirement behind this request. They suggested that it was probably in order to track shells etc. to determine either firing point or point of impact. A complete series of measurements had been made at 50 cms. on full scale models of shells of calibres 21 and 28 cms and on Russian mortar bombs. The technique used was very sound. The models were placed on wooden poles so that the received and transmitted beams could be inclined at 45 degs so as to avoid ground reflections, and to avoid standing waves - a frequency modulation of $\pm 1\%$ was used. Various inclinations and polarisations were used and the received signals were compared with a λ^2 plate in each case. Some sample curves were taken away.

It was discovered in one of the technical files in Prof. Gorcke's laboratory that trials at Grosshorn with a Wurzburg D and a Wurzburg-Riese had been carried out in Nov. 1944 with field artillery and with 15, 21 and 30 cms mortars. The results had proved interesting and according to the minutes of the meeting at Grosshorn, the services were asking for a development of a radar giving a range of 50-100 Km. on shells and at least 100 Km on enemy artillery weapons. The B.H.F. representative pointed out the impossibility of this with present technique. Instructions had been given to continue the trials at Grosshorn. The polar diagram work at the institute was clearly associated with these trials.

The programme of work on these polar diagrams had included further work at 80, 10 and 3 cms. but the interruptions due to the evacuation had prevented a start being made. No report had been prepared.

Dr. Breuning did not know definitely of any similar work at other institutes but he thought that some work on the same lines was being done by Prof. Braun at Peenemunde.

The work on reflections from rocket gases had again been carried out at the request of the B.H.F. but without any concrete idea of the operational requirement. Prof. Gorcke suggested that it was in order to check whether it was possible for our radar (Rotterdam) to detect the firing points but Prof. Scherzer when interrogated had stated that this work on reflections was to establish if any errors in radar tracking were introduced by the hot gases.

An interim report on the work had been prepared (Zwischen-versuchsberielt No.1) and a copy has been taken away. Most of this work was done at 9.3 cms. but observations have also been made with both larger and shorter wavelengths. A nebelwerfer was used to produce the flame and was set up on the ground so that the flame was vertical. The transmitting and receiving mirrors were chosen to be of diameter approximately equal to the width of the flame and were placed at 2 and a $\frac{1}{2}$ metres from the flame.

Some interesting results were obtained but further experiments were needed to clear up some inconsistencies as well as to study the effect of polarisation, frequency etc. The polarisation used was horizontal but it appeared that a uniform polar diagram was obtained for the scattered radiation in the horizontal plane. The amplitude of the scattered radiation was equivalent to that from a 50 x 50 cm. metal plate at normal incidence and was about four times that from the nebilwerfer body itself (presumably at normal incidence).

Preliminary experiments with other frequencies indicated that the proportion of radiation from the gas to that from the nebilwerfer body increased at high frequencies.

It was mentioned that some attempts to detect a V2 with a Rotterdam equipment had been made at Karlshagen Nr. Peenemunde in March 1944 and that the nil results obtained were in some way associated with the exhaust gases.

Reflection tests had also been made on incendiary bombs and smoke bombs. The general result was that reflections were only obtained from the actual jet of flame.

This laboratory had also undertaken experiments at Luneburg, Nr. Hamburg on detection of panzers from the air with an H2S apparatus. These experiments were demanded apparently by the

Wehrmacht. It was thought that the Oberpfaffenhofen laboratories had been developing special equipment for detection of panzers.

This Abteilung No.2 had also handled a sketchy programme on pulse modulated jammers and search receivers.

The construction of a high power pulse modulated jammer was started in the autumn of 1944 at the request of the B.H.F. The design was never completed owing to the fact that S band tubes of sufficiently high output were not available, but the modulator was designed and constructed and trials at lower power levels made. The equipment was to consist of a 1000 Kw 6 Kc PRF rotary spark gap modulator, magnetron oscillator and biconical horn antenna.

The horn main lobe was aimed towards the ground in order that the A/c would receive not only direct radiation but also that reflected from the ground and thus achieve a more random effort.

Trials were made using 100 Kws (LMS 100) against an airborne Rotterdam unit. No quantitative observations were made but the method was considered to be effective. The equipment tunes through a small range by adjustment of magnetic field and plate voltages. This was considered adequate since Prof. Gorcke's measurements indicated that 80% of H2S equipments operated at 9.18 cm. The equipment was not used operationally.

Other R.C.M. work

The institute requested and received a Carpet I from the enemy equipment pool at Kothen. This unit was to be analysed with a view toward development of A.I. devices. The first step in this direction was an attempt to find holes in the frequency spectrum but their technique was inadequate and the project was dropped. It seems that this organisation received no reports on analyses of this Carpet unit and the project was started only because of personal interest without any B.H.F. requests

Various other types of R.C.M. equipment were on hand in the laboratories including Roderich, Korfu, Samos, Fanve and Naxos. This latter unit was used at the laboratory to measure the distribution of H2S frequencies in a/c of bombing missions flying over the laboratory.

This laboratory designed some rather rudimentary "search receivers" for wave lengths around 1 cm, each consisting of a conical horn leading to rectangular wave guide fitted with a small probe and crystal.

Mention was made that Naxos receivers were used with paraboloids on about a 50 to 60 Km layout to plot the course of H2S fitted aircraft.

This laboratory had also made measurements on the reflection coefficients of wood, water, salt solutions and samples of absorbing paper from I.G. Farben. The measurements on the absorbing paper are not quoted as the figures were only produced from memory as no report had been prepared.

There is no doubt that Prof. Gorcke is a very capable physicist, but it would seem that owing to lack of direction from either the B.H.F. or Dr. Breuning he had dissipated his efforts in a series of unrelated researches.

Beyharting Laboratories: These 'laboratories' consisted of a room in the upper floor of the gasthaus and an odd room in the school. The equipment had merely been dumped into these laboratories. It had been intended that these would be the laboratories of division 3.

Dr. Herold, a physicist and a section leader in this division was interrogated thoroughly. He spoke quite good English. Before joining the institute at the end of 1943 he had worked in the Luftwaffe on fitting out aircraft and submarines with search receivers and had been an assistant of Prof. Scherzer in N.Africa and the Meditteranean. He had installed and tested a Wanz gerat - a search receiver for 160-220 mcs - on a U boat - and related how the distance away of our A.S.V. equipped aircraft was estimated by the height of the signal on a C.R.T. Later it appeared that the ASV. transmitter power was reduced and this completely upset the method of use. He had helped to build A.S.V. jammers in the Meditteranean (in Sicily Crete etc.) and a number of other jammers. When asked why certain particular modulations were used (e.g. F.M. on 25 mc/s, 300 kc/s on other frequencies) he stated that the Luftwaffe (Gen. Martini) had ordered that jammers to such a specification be built and as a junior physicist he had to do as he was told. He knew that an airborne survey of radar frequencies was carried out over Southern England in 1940 to 1941 and he himself had made measurements from an E boat off Hull. He could not remember any of the results as he had prepared no reports and had given his report verbally after each mission. He stated that the ground jammers used at Boulogne and Sicily were operated by technical officers of the Luftwaffe but he did not think that they knew much about the job.

-203-

The division in which Dr. Herold worked had carried out numerous A.J. investigations. They appear to have been responsible for the initial circuiting for the Freya-laus in order to combat window and permanent echoes. A complete report, some 39 pages and circuit diagrams, has been taken away (Versuchsbericht No.14). This report includes the early history and difficulties of the Freya-laus development and also a report on anti-clutter tests made in mountainous districts. They claimed fair success for the Freya-laus. The trials were carried out at Gatow, which was regarded as an out-station and trials centre (abteilung). This division I has also issued a report on the development of a similar phase-regulating oscillator for the Mannheim-Vollwismar. It was not clear why this work was carried out as Telefunken had already developed a Tastlaus for the B and C frequencies. This new circuit was presumably for the A frequency as well. A copy of the report on this work has been taken away (Versuchszwischenbericht No.12)

Dr. Herold had been working on an interesting though probably rather impracticable type of anti-window presentation. The aim was to display both range and radial velocity. No report has been prepared and so this proposal was discussed in some detail. Successive time base sweeps are presented one above the other to form a raster. The raster frequency used was 20 c.p.s. The sweep is intensity modulated. A saw tooth frequency modulated coherent oscillator sweeps from some value below the transmitter frequency to about the same amount above. This F.M. is synchronised with the raster sweep. A target, it was claimed, now appears as a diagonal line which becomes a vertical line when the coho frequency is the same as the received frequency. Thus for stationary targets this occurs at the centre of the raster and for targets with varying radial velocities at different levels on the raster. Some preliminary experiments had been made and although Dr. Herold was quite enthusiastic, the investigating team could not see any grounds for enthusiasm.

The 'laboratory' at the Gasthaus contained a miscellaneous collection of Freya and Lichtenstein parts, signal generators, oscilloscopes, some photographic equipment, tools, etc. The 'laboratory' at the school contained a quantity of absorbent paper (corrugated paper, metal foil backed) supplied by I.G.Farben, a polyrod antenna mounted on a Rotterdam spinner and a great deal of junk.

Schalldorf laboratories.

This was some six miles from Beyharting and contained the remnants of Maier's division 4. The staff, in two rooms above a gasthaus, were busily engaged on repairing local broadcast receivers (presumably in order to earn their board and lodging).

This division had completed when at Ulm a series of propellor modulation studies at 9 cms. but had never completed the analysis of the results. The purpose of the work was not clear. It appeared to be a B.H.F. request but no attempt had been made to compare the signal from the propellor with that of the fuselage. An RD2MC magnetron modulated at 100 kc/s was used. The photographic records show a fairly steady signal at exactly normal incidence and at 90 degs. Between 10 degs. and 30 degs. four peaks appeared per revolution, but only two per revolution from 40 degs. to 80 degs. The propellor was a two-blade metal one.

This laboratory had started the construction of a Window simulator using a water delay tank. It was proposed to produce bubbles in the water by electrolysis and this to represent Window. There would seem little purpose in this experiment except as a trainer.

Like many other labs. this one had also constructed a jammer for Rotterdam using an RD2MC, eventually tuned with a balanced line and shorting bar. The life of the tube was stated to be some 8 hours after which the cathode disintegrated. There was also in this lab. a nullschlitsrohr complete with magnet and external tuning, covering from 3 - 10 cms. It had been constructed by the FFO, Oberpfaffenhofen and engineers were to have come to set it up and demonstrate. It had accordingly never been used.

Jakobsburg Laboratories: These comprised a couple of rooms in farm buildings, one of the 'rooms' being a small cow-shed. It was referred to as the chemical and high vacuum laboratories but at present it comprises mainly junk. Attempts had been made to repair magnetrons in the vacuum laboratory at Ulm and to make crystals. There seemed some doubt about the value of the reconstructed magnetrons but no doubt at all that the crystals they had constructed were not as good as Telefunken's. Two pre-treatment ovens and some pumps indicated that the Institute probably had a reasonably good high vacuum plant at Ulm but it would have been quite impracticable to have set up and worked in these farm buildings.

Schmitthausen store: In a barn were contained field telephones, cables, instruments of various types etc. still in packing cases.

Schlachtham workshop: This was again part of a farm building and contained 4 lathes, 2 drilling machines, 1 miller and 1 shaper, none of which was of particular value. These machines had never been installed and no work had been done by the staff since the evacuation.

Bad Aibling store: On the third floor of the Schulbrau all the component stores had been dumped. There was nothing of technical interest here but it indicates that the store at Ulm was probably quite well equipped.

Holzhausen store: This store was not visited. It was stated that it contained nothing more than cables, parts of Wurzburgs, Freyas, etc.

After seeing 7 out of 8 of these evacuation centres it was considered that it would have been more or less impracticable for the Institute to have carried out any satisfactory work under such conditions.

SECTION D

REPORTS ISSUED BY THE Z V H.

Versuchsbericht No.1 - Range control of HS293
" 2 - Null positions of directional antennae
" 3 - Use of HS293 and FX in the channel area
" 4 - Use of a frequency changer of ± 3 Mc/s for airborne and ground radars.
" 5 - Polar Diagrams of the Sn2 on the JU88 and HeIII
" 6 - Die relative Vergrosserung des Pegelverhält- nisses durch periodische Basisverschiebung bei Fu M. geraten.
" 7 - Phase shifters and their calibration.
" 8 - Investigation of the Rotterdam pulse unit.
" 9 - Impulse transmitter for ultra-sonic work.
" 10 - Report on British and American receivers.
" 11 - Application of the converter ST.W.3 and of the quasi-static voltmeter.
" 12 - Report on radar method "Bar".
" 13 - Production of impulses from a sine wave.
" 14 - Development and investigation of A.J. methods for Freya against clutter and Window.
" 15 - Carrier transmission of P.P.I. pictures.

<u>Versuchszwischenbericht</u> No.1 - Detection of rocket gases.

    "   2 - Reflection of cm. waves from various materials.

    "   3 - Detection of conducting material embedded in partially conducting material (mine detection)

    "   4 - Investigations on captured detectors.

    "   5 - Evaluation of Rotterdam pictures.

    "   6 - Possibility of D/F on large calibre rockets.

    "   7 - Investigation of the possibility of jamming Rotterdam type of equipment.

    "   8 - Reduction of ground clutter.

    "   9 - Observations on enemy technique.

    "   10 - Jamming of Rotterdam presentation by transmitter on same frequency and higher P.R.F. using indirect reflection.

    "   11 - Investigation of enemy detectors.

Of these complete and interim reports, the following are being forwarded to C.I.O.S.

Versuchsbericht 1,2,3,4,5,7,8,9,11,13,14,15.

Versuchszwischenbericht 1,2,3,5,7,9,10,11.

The missing numbers were said to have been lost.

SECTION E.

List of the Scientific personnel belonging to the Institute and now in the Bad Aibling area (Mechanics female lab. assts. clerks etc. not included).

Dr. Breuning,	Dipl. Ing.
Voelkil	Dipl. Ing.
Prof. Gorcke,	Dipl. Ing.
Maier,	
Dr. Herold,	Physicist.
Bachhuber.	Ing.
Dolker,	Dipl. Ing.
Fenzl,	Dipl. Ing.
Godde,	Ing.
Kammerer,	Dipl. Ing.
Klimper,	Ing.
Nuss,	Ing.
Oesterlein.	Ing.
Flossea,	Ing.
Dr. Schultzer,	Physicist.
Schumacher,	Dipl. Ing
Voigt,	Ing.
Schneider,	Dipl. Ing
Averdung,	Dipl. Ing.
Gerber	Ing.
Romisch,	Ing.
Zemaneh	Ing.
Funk,	Ing.
Vollmer,	Stud. physicist.
Oldach,	Ing.
Filipowcky	Dipl. Ing.
Lier,	Ing.
Pilz,	Dipl. Ing.
Dordelmann,	Dipl. Ing.
Forster,	Dipl. Ing.
Dr. Schodder,	Chemist.
Dr. Trant,	Chemist
Dr. Peschen,	Physicist.
Kepfer,	Ing.
Berggold,	Ing.
Dr. Durst,	Physicist.
Frerichs,	Ing
Kuhnel,	Dipl. Ing.
Pfluger	Dipl. Ing.
Schirmer	Dipl. Ing
Rosenkranz	Ing.
Stochel,	Ing.
Wiskemann,	Ing.

SECTION F.

ACTION TAKEN.

232 C.P. and Military government, Bad Aibling were given, in writing, a short assessment value of the dispersal centres. It was stated that no equipment of intelligence or military value was contained in any of the laboratories or stores and there was no reason to continue the guards on two of the stores.

All the staff, including Dr. Breuning, were very anxious to return to their homes at Ulm. All were referred to military government.

A complete list of all the staff in the Bad Aibling area, including mechanics, clerks etc. was handed to Military Government, Bad Aibling.

Georg Simon Institute, Murnau.

Interrogation of Dr. Nelting

Investigators:
- Mr. C.W. Hansell — T.I.I.C.
- Capt. M. Snowden — R.R.D.E.

Address of George Simon Institute
Cafe Seeblick, Murnau

Address of Dr. Nelting.
1, Philosopher Weg, Murnau.

Report on Interrogation

The original Institute was at Heidelberg and employed about 20 people in all. The principal was Dr. Gottpied Eckhardt.

12 people in all were evacuated to Murnau the technical members of which were:
- Dr. Gottpied Eckhardt
- Dr. Heinz Netling
- Dr. Otto Franke
- Erhard Pfister
- Dr. Viktor Fetzer - Loaned from Mix and Geust of Berlin.
- Adolf Kubring - A Mathematician.

Dr. Eckhardt was taken prisoner by local Polish troops. The remaining 5 technicians were still at Murnau.

The Cafe Seeblick was only a small place and no work had been done there. Three crates of apparatus were opened by assessors who visited the Cafe previous to us. None of the apparatus was of interest.

Nelting said that most of their equipment had been lost due to Allied action during their evacuation.

The work of the institute had been concerned chiefly with the measurement of the dielectric constant and conductivity of pure water lake water and various samples of earth. Measurements had been made at D.C. and at frequencies up to 10 Mc/s.

More recently they had been ordered to do measurements at centimeter wavelengths and had only just started to collect the necessary apparatus when they had to evacuate from Heidelberg. Centimetre valves for these measurements had been received but the type numbers of the valves were not known by either Nelting or Dr. Otto Franke who was called in to verify some of Nelting's statements. Franke was very nervous and did not seem to be very intelligent.

The purpose of these measurements was to study the propogation and reflection of R.F. waves. Progress reports on this and other work were said to have been written but lost during evacuation.

In addition some work on wide band I.F. amplifiers had been done. All this work was centered on an I.F. frequency of 10 Mc/s and the band widths concerned were only 2 and 4 Mc/s. Staggering of the tuned circuits had been investigated and the mathematics of such circuits worked out in detail. The Telefunken pentode type E.F.14 had been used in these amplifiers.

It was stated that the wide band amplifiers were built to study the build-up of oscillations and no knowledge of their use for a military application was admitted. No reports on this work were available.

Nelting stated that they had done no work on communication systems of any kind. He stated however that Mix and Geust produced such equipment.

Conclusions:

Very little useful work had been done by this Institute. It is possible that Eckhardt might help to fill in the gaps between the information about the Institute obtained in Heidelberg and that furnished by Nelting and Franke. The staff was very small and of limited ability judging by Nelting and Franke.

Nelting was anxious to obtain M.G. permission to start work again and reorganise his laboratory. We advised him to grow potatoes.

C.W. Hansell.
M. Snowden.

29th May, 1945.

Reichstelle fur Hochfrequenzforschung Hamburg.

LOCATION: Isekai, Hamburg.

DATE: 12 July, 1945

REMARKS: This target was visited to obtain the address of a Reichstelle fur H.F. research in Schleswig supposedly under the direction of a Prof. Brandi. Dr. Mohr of this institute knew nothing of Reichstelle. The only H.F. Institutes he knew of were the ones at Hamburg and Travemunde. These two institutes are shortly to be renamed and combined at Eppendorfer Krankenhaus, Barracks 25, Hamburg, there to undertake medical research as a University Department. Prof. Brandi is stated to be a Professor of Architecture and to know nothing of H.F. research. He is being transferred to Gottingen University.

Apparently the following institutes are being renamed in some cases and all made responsible to Universities.

1. Hochfrequenz Technisches Institute in der Fa. Guericke G.M.B.H. of Preetz.
2. Hochfrequenz Inst. Travemunde.
3. Hochfrequenz Inst. Hamburg.
4. Max Wien Inst. Bergedorf.
5. Astron. Inst. der Hansischen Universitat.
6. Ernst Orlich Inst. of Danzig.

Details of all these changes have been sent to F/Lt. Holt CAFT Group I 21 A.G. The following changes of address may not, however, be known:

1. Dr. Kroebel formerly of Hagenuk now at Bredeneek near Preetz.
2. Dr. Roewer formerly of Ernst Orlich Inst. now at universitat Kiel.
3. Dr. Netheler head of Travemunde Inst. now at 14-18 Rosengarten Lubeck.

Investigator - S/Ldr. G.C. Barker, M.A.P.

Reichsstelle fur Hochfrequenzforschung Schleswig.

REMARKS:

All efforts to find this target failed. Enquiries as to the location were made at

1. T Force Hamburg, Kiel and Stohl.
2. High Frequency Institutes at Isequai, Hamburg and Schloss Bredeneck, Preetz.
3. Military Government, Civil Police and Kiel University in Schleswig.

None of these places had any knowledge of this target. It seems fair to assume that this target does not exist.

Investigator :- S/Ldr. G.C. Barker,   M.A.P.

www.ingramcontent.com/pod-product-compliance
Lightning Source LLC
Chambersburg PA
CBHW080411230426
43662CB00016B/2371